D0509803

PRINT CASEBOOKS 10/
THE BEST IN ENVIRONMENTAL GRAPHICS

CALIFORNIA COLLEGE OF ARTS AND CRAFTS
ARCHITECTURE
WITHDRA
COLLECTION
MEYER LIBRARY

PRINT
CASEBOOKS 10
THE BEST IN
ENVIRONMENTAL
GRAPHICS

WITHDRAWN

CALIFORNIA COLLEGE OF ARTS AND CRAFTS
ARCHITECTURE
COLLECTION
MEYER LIBRARY

Written by
Akiko Busch
Published by
RC Publications, Inc., Rockville, MD

Copyright © 1994 by RC Publications, Inc. All rights reserved.

First published in 1994 in the United States of America by RC Publications, Inc. 3200 Tower Oaks Boulevard Rockville, MD 20852

No part of this publication may be reproduced or used in any form or by any means—graphic, electronic, or mechanical, including photocopying, recording, taping, or information storage and retrieval systems—without written permission of the publisher.

Manufactured in Singapore

First Printing 1994

PRINT CASEBOOKS 10/THE BEST IN ENVIRONMENTAL GRAPHICS (1994–95 EDITION)
Library of Congress Catalog Card Number 75-649581
ISBN 0-915734-90-7

PRINT CASEBOOKS 10 (1994–95 EDITION)
Complete 6-Volume Set
ISBN 0-915734-87-7

RC PUBLICATIONS
President and Publisher: Howard Cadel
Vice President and Editor: Martin Fox
Managing Director: Linda Silver
Art Director: Andrew P. Kner
Assistant Art Director: Michele L. Trombley
Copy Editor: Seth Greene
Cover Illustration: Brian Ajhar

Inevitably, the projects not voted into this Casebook offer more, or perhaps just more obvious, lessons than those that are. As in the past, this year's jurors commented on the number of imperfect submissions, those with agendas that were in one way or another unrealized. Because environmental graphics touches so many other design disciplines—architecture, interior design, and landscape design, among them—jurors frequently felt that some part of a program simply didn't live up to the rest. These programs, for the most part, did not make it into this Casebook.

If the success of an environmental graphics program has to do with how things add up, jurors found that, in the unsuccessful programs, typography was most often the inconsistent component. When other graphic elements seemed considered and integrated into the whole, the typography seemed an afterthought. This was a fatal flaw, as were the wavy lines. Once a trend used on everything from menus to signage, this series of wavy lines now comes off as a stylistic tic designers can't shake.

That said, what were the other repeated flaws? Dubbed "food court fatigue" by the jurors, the plastic quality of mall and food-court iconography challenged their stamina. This area can seriously use help. As mail-order catalogs and the electronic marketplace increasingly compete with shopping malls, designers are going to be asked more often to make the mall an appealing and engaging place. The evidence among this year's submissions, however, suggested that for the moment the mall remains a bland and homogenized landscape: Seattle could be Tampa could be Pittsburgh. Few regional references, few local acknowledgements, and few indigenous materials were used.

When there was an exception, it was the wrong kind. Jurors responded with outright disbelief at one shopping mall program that took the local Amish tradition as its inspiration—if you could call it that. While the designers received points for selecting a regional theme, connecting the austere values of this religious group to the commercialism of shopping malls seems inappropriate, if not outright insensitive.

In response to the homogeneity that prevailed among so many submissions, juror Jon Roll made the case for research: "When you have a context, you should do your research and run with it. The research is fun." Whether it means researching regional traditions, local landmarks, or indigenous materials, all the jurors made an appeal for designers in this category to get to know and use the specifics of their site, building, and the environment. Indeed, many entries were voted into the Casebook exactly because the designers had made that effort.

Another problem the jurors repeatedly saw, as in past years, was that most designers haven't yet found a way to incorporate electronic signage into their programs. Can't LCD displays, for example, be integrated with traditional materials such as stone and bronze? Indeed, shouldn't such integration be a creative challenge to the profession?

Also disappointing was the shared dearth of social awareness among many of the submissions. Where were the recycled materials? Where was the green? Most surprising was the minor recognition given to the mandates of the Americans with Disabilities Act (ADA), signed into law in 1990. Most entries were completed before the ADA implementation guidelines, so design solutions to ADA mandates were still unnecessary. Disappointingly, though, numerous entry applications gave the distinct impression that designers were doing their best to get in under the wire; many seemed obviously relieved to complete their programs before being confined by this oppressive legislation.

And this was discouraging. How much more encouraging it would have been to find designers using ADA legislation as the creative incentive to find ways in which graphics and signage might make public spaces more accessible to more people. The size and position of lettering, use of color and texture, the braille alphabet, for example, are all graphic elements that can make a design statement. They can also bring a sense of humanity to a building or public space.

What, then, were the high points in this year's submissions? In the words of juror Jon Roll, "This was a great year for donor walls." By their nature, donor walls appear in places that usually don't have big budgets. This year, in particular, the consistent creativity shown in donor-recognition systems underscored the fact that budget constraints are often what generate the greatest innovation.

Then there was the humor. Throughout many entries was evidence that designers and clients alike are willing to take themselves less seriously. Irony at an annual shareholders' convention, mouse ears that aspire to elegance, a salad bowl the size of a house—these programs and others demonstrate the sense of invention that comes from taking oneself lightly.

But the brightest points among the 1500 or so slides were those celebrating the beauty of the ordinary. If there was any single approach that marked the entries that really stood out, it was this appreciation for the average. In the '90s, extravagence is a thing of the past. (As juror Ken Carbone put it, "A lot of money in the hands of the wrong designer can be a terrible thing.") So, instead, jurors were offered a cup of coffee elevated to sainthood; and a golf tee produced as an immense machine-age sculpture. Such transformations of the ordinary can't help but capture the imagination. If these submissions issued a directive, it was about the beautiful possibilities of taking common,

utiliarian icons and going someplace with them.

Maintaining a tradition of this Casebook, these comments must close with an appeal for clear language. Designer jargon is getting out of hand—way out of hand. "Pedestrian experience" isn't a phrase that says much to anyone, inside or outside the profession; "visitor-friendly environment" isn't much better. And the jurors could not take seriously entry forms that referred to walkway or street intersections as "decision-making points." If designers want people to understand what they do, expressing themselves clearly might be a good place to start.

—*Akiko Busch*

Akiko Busch

A graduate of Bennington College, Akiko Busch has written about architecture, design, and crafts in trade journals for 15 years. She is also a contributing editor of Metropolis magazine.

She has served as a staff editor at Residential Interiors and Metropolis magazines, and as guest editor for ID's annual design reviews and the Print Casebooks on environmental graphics. Busch has also written catalog essays for several exhibitions at the American Craft Museum. Her books include *The Photography of Architecture* , *The Art of the Architectural Model, Wallworks, Floorworks,* and, most recently, *Rooftop Architecture: The Art of Going through the Roof.*

James Biber

James Biber graduated with honors from Cornell University's College of Architecture, Art, and Planning. He was the senior associate with Paul Segal Associates in New York before forming James Biber Architect in 1984. In 1991, he joined the New York office of Pentagram as a partner; there he established Pentagram Architectural Services.

Among Biber's varied projects are New York residences, restaurants, showrooms, and offices. His work has been recognized consistently by awards from the New York State Association of Architects, the New York Chapter of the AIA, the IDSA, the Municipal Art Society, and the Architectural League. He has also taught at Cornell University, Syracuse University, and Parsons School of Design.

Kenneth Carbone

Kenneth Carbone is a designer and principal of Carbone Smolan Associates in New York City, a graphic design firm well known for its work in visitor information systems, exhibitions, identity development, print, and architectural graphics. His award-winning projects have been recognized by AIGA, Print Casebooks, Graphis, IDEA, Communication Arts, and the New York Art Directors Club. His work is included in the permanent collection of the Cooper-Hewitt Museum in New York City.

Carbone has also been a visiting lecturer in graphic design at Yale, Rhode Island School of Design, Carnegie Mellon University, and the University of Washington. A member of AIGA, he served as a past treasurer of its New York chapter.

Virginia Gehshan

An honors graduate of Cornell University, Virginia Gehshan was a graphic designer for five years at Philadelphia's Noel Mayo Associates, then served as director of graphic design for three years at Daroff Design, Inc., also in Philadelphia. She started her own firm in 1983 and became partners with Jerome Cloud in 1986.

Cloud and Gehshan Associates, Inc. creates identification programs, marketing communications, and architectural signage. The firm's work has been recognized by AIGA, Graphis, Print Casebooks, ID magazine, SEGD, and Identity magazine.

Gehshan has also served as president of SEGD. She has taught graphic design for eight years at the University of the Arts and has lectured widely to professional and student audiences.

Jon T. Roll

After earning a B.A. from Dartmouth, Jon Roll worked as a designer with the Hopkins Center Design Associates. After serving in the U.S. Army in Vietnam, he was a Rabinowitz Fellow at Pratt Institute, earning an M.S. in design and working as design director of the Student Design Studios.

Since 1973, he has specialized in architectural and environmental design. Prior to forming his own firm, he worked for Gumaelius Annonsbyro in Stockholm; Walter Thompson de Mexico in Mexico City; and Cuellar, Serrano, Gomez in Bogota, Colombia. He was also responsible for environmental design at Herman and Lees Associates in Cambridge, Massachusetts.

In recent years, Roll has designed and implemented sign systems throughout the world. He also speaks frequently on the applications of environmental graphics and computer graphics.

Index Projects

Clients Sponsoring Organizations

Designers
Architects
Consultants

Adam, Peter **51**
Alderfer, Hannah **22**
Ambrosini, Kenneth G. **14**
Arata Isoyaki & Associates **60**
Ash, Stuart **51**
Ashton, David **57**
Ashton, David, and Co., Ltd. **57**
Bailey, Craig **66**
Bangor, Beth **86**
Barnes, Edward
Larrabee/Lee, John M.Y., &
Associates **68**
Berman, Susan **63**
Berns Farrow
Architects, Inc. **27**
Biber, James **30**
Bierut, Michael **30**
Birdsall, Connie **27**
Bliss, Pam **90**
Blocksom, Dutro **24**
Bond, Anne **12**
Boyd Associates **20**
Brabo, Allan **12**
Bricker, John **83**
Burak, Larry **51**
Cambridge Seven
Associates **44**
Carbone Smolan Associates
10, 86
Carbone, Kenneth **86**
Castellan, Diane **51**
Cerveney, Lisa **30**
Chermayeff & Geismar **44**
Chermayeff, Ivan **44**
Ching, Donna **75**
Chwast, Seymour **88**
Cieradkowski, Gary **57**
Cincinnati, City of, Office of
Architecture, Graphic Design
Section **24**
Colvin, Alan **12**
Crone, Joanne **51**
Curran, Laura **24**
Cuyler, Scott **41,72**
Dentsu, Inc. **75**
Design Partnership **14**
Dinkeloo, John, &

Associates **63**
Donovan and Green **63**
Donovan, Michael **63**
Drodville, Debra **68**
Drummond, Scott **66**
Eisenman, Peter **54**
Elder, Richard **12**
Ellenzweig Associates **38**
Ellison, Joan **27**
Forbes, Colin **75**
Frankfurt Balkind Partners **54**
Frueh, Lucy **24**
Geismar, Tom **44**
Gensler and Associates/
Architects **83**
Gensler and Associates/
Graphics **83**
Gericke, Michael **75**
Giles, Robin **54**
Gloar, Gena **12**
Gottschalk+Ash
International **51**
Graham Gund Architects **17**
Hampton, Holly **72**
Helmetag, Keith **44**
Hellmuth, Obata,
Kassabaum **57**
Henrekin, Theresa **90**
Horton Lees Lighting
Design **83**
Horton, Tom **83**
Houston Visual
Committee, The **22**
Hunter, Kent **54**
Intra Design, Inc. **75**
Jensen, Robert **51**
Johnson, Randy **51**
Juett, Dennis S., &
Associates, Inc. **36**
Juett, Dennis Scott **36**
Keane, James **90**
Ketchen, Robert **51**
Kohn Pedersen Fox Interior
Architects **10**
Koman, Jessica **57**
Kotch, Rebecca **12**
Kovats, Katlin **51**

Krivanek, B. J. **33**
Krivanek, B.J., Art+Design **33**
Landor Associates **94**
Legorreta, Ricardo **72**
Lighting Management, Inc. **90**
Lippincott & Margulies,
Inc. **27**
Loetterle, Ruth **48**
Lugar, Denise **17**
Mankowski, Michael **12**
Mantels-Seeker, Ed **90**
Manzilli, R.P., & Co. **48**
Martin, Laura **24**
McGinnis Shortt, Marcia **24**
McGinty, Idie **90**
McGinty, Tim **90**
McNeely, Jane **90**
Melandri, Michelle **12**
Morla Design **66**
Morla, Jennifer **66**
Moskin, Tina **54**
Muller, Keith **51**
Muller, Keith, and
Associates **51**
Nelson, Marybeth **22**
Nike Design **12**
Nishimoto, John **86**
O'Dowd, Rachel **94**
Obata, Kiku & Co. **90**
Obata, Kiku **90**
Oman, Sarah **54**
OUN Design Corp. **75**
Pentagram Design:New York
30, 75
Poelvoorde, Raymond **27**
Poulin, Richard **68**
Poulin, Richard, Design
Group, Inc. **68**
Poulson, Randy **12**
Pushpin Group, Inc., The **88**
Retson, Corky **72**
Richardson, Robert H. **24**
Rieger, David **33**
Roberts, Susan **20**
Roberts, Susan: Art Color
Design **20**
Roche, Kevin **63**

Rohrer, Denise **24**
Roll, Jon **38**
Roll, Jon, & Associates **17,38**
Rudie, Nelson **90**
Rumbaugh, Joan,
Engineering **48**
Schaefer, Cathy **44**
Schrager, Sara **27**
Selbert, Clifford **48**
Selbert, Clifford, Design **48**
Shoemaker, Laurel **54**
Skidmore, Owings &
Merrill **41**
Slimach, Roxanne **88**
Snodgrass, Ric **24**
Stafford, Sharon **38**
Steinorth, Kirsten **68**
Sussman, Deborah **41,72**
Sussman/Prejza & Co., Inc.
41,72
Thompson Vaivoda &
Associates **14**
Thompson, Gordon **12**
Tong, Brenda **51**
Tonizzo, David **51**
Turner, Tracy **60**
Turner, Tracy, Design **60**
Uden, Graham **60**
Van Verspoor, Wayne **27**
Vogel, Julie **83**
Voorsanger and Associates **86**
Walt Disney Imagineering **78**
Walt Disney Imagineering,
Graphic Design Department,
Mickey's Toontown Team **78**
Walt Disney Imagineering,
Architecture Department,
Mickey's Toontown Team **78**
Weil, Rafael **17**
Wilson, Allen **63**
Wong, Robert **54**
Wuest, M.J. **17**
Youngblood, Margaret **94**
Zweck-Bronner, Michael **30**

The designers explain that "The curvilinear forms [of this signage program] were inspired by the unique office interior." To say the least; the interior is distinguished, indeed animated, by an unusual architectural component, an undulating glass wall that defines the perimeter of the office space. Dubbed "the wiggle wall," the wavy structure has a sandblasted surface, which allows for both illumination and privacy. Handrails used in the interior follow a similar curve, and the office's custom-designed desks feature a wavy wood panel in front. Not surprisingly, then, the designers envisioned the graphics program as three-dimensional.

"We looked at forms, volume, and scale from the start," they say of their program, which throws yet another lively curve into the corporate interior. Indeed, the sculptural format of the main identity sign sets the tone for what is to come. Constructed from formed and painted acrylic with three-dimensional constructed brass lettering, the 19'-tall sign flows down a two-story atrium and features a gentle curve consistent with the architectural elements. Predictably, fabricating such a large form presented problems: because the acrylic panels could only fit in the oven diagonally, the sign was ultimately constructed in two parts and fused on site. Still, the first two attempts failed as the panels cracked en route.

The program also included less monumental elements, such as wall and glass-

1.

mounted personnel signs, freestanding desk-top signs, wall-mounted room identity signs, and code and informational panels. The materials specified for these were determined by their availability, cost, and ease in maintaining, replacing, and re-ordering. Brass was used for all fittings and stands, and all copy was screened either flat or on raised polymer forms. Flexible vinyl was used for changeable name panels; brass attachments with small screws hold the curved panels in place, with the curve of each determined by the placement of its attachment. The designers emphasized their efforts to be innovative without being indulgent, and the Casebook jurors agreed that the sense of economy used in specifying such materials and construction techniques allowed them to be just that.

Bauer Bodoni Book was the typeface used throughout the program. The sign panels themselves are off-white, and all primary copy is maroon—the client's corporate identity color and one it felt should be prominent. Black was specified for all secondary copy because it was readable and did not compete with the maroon.

"There was a strong architectural vision as well as a rich palette of materials to be inspired by," the designers conclude. "Our mission was to be seamless with that vision." While they clearly accomplished their goal, what is just as noteworthy is that they did it with such an efficient and cost-effective program.

2.   3.   4.

5.

1. *Sculptural identity sign in atrium.*
2. *Wall-mounted code and information panel.*
3. *Room identity sign.*
4. *Free-standing desktop sign repeats wave form.*
5. *Wall-mounted room identity sign.*

Client: FGIC, New York, NY
Design firm: Carbone Smolan Associates, New York, NY
Architect: Kohn Pederson Fox Interior Architects, New York, NY
Fabricator: ASI Sign System, New York, NY

Nike Town Store and Construction Barricade

The Casebook jurors found the construction barricade that hid the site of Chicago's new Nike Town store and the store's own graphics program equally engaging. Both programs were based on a consistent message of lively animation that accurately reflects the spirit of the company.

Begin with the 80'-long, plywood construction barricade, which set the tone for the retail store to come. The barricade's interactive graphics combined cut-out 6'-high letters in Futura Condensed Extra Bold with back-lighting on its walkway, to create the illusion that pedestrians were actually passing through Nike Town. In the painted plywood mural above the colonnade, an assembly of lifesize athletes appeared to be mounted on a stylized coach's locker-room play board. The palette of black, white, and Nike's corporate PMS Warm Red reiterated the sense of drama.

While the barricade clearly announced the impending store opening, it also conveyed the sense of animated athletic fun used to promote Nike's products.

Move onto the store itself. The graphic element that most impressed jurors inside the three-story, 30,000-square-foot retail space was the floor, perceived by the designers as "a 3-D marketing and communications tool for Nike's various collections." Product, archival, and merchandising displays, product-information stations, and environmental signage were all designed right into the floor and expressed in a variety of materials including wood, terrazzo, and sandstone. The realization of this floor required designers to research new technologies and materials as well as work collaboratively with the architects throughout its design, construction, and installation.

The patterning of the terrazzo floor of the International Pavilion took its cues from the globe: latitude and longitude lines, as well as the four compass points, give pattern and color. In the Tennis Pavilion, the terrazzo floor is superimposed with tennis court lines, though at a skewed angle. Tennis balls, complete with their shadows, add further dimension to the pattern. In the Men's Fitness Pavilion, the designers adopted the imagery of old gymnasiums and installed a section of yellow pine flooring. The Women's Pavilion, on the other hand, relies on the softer, more sensual imagery, of large spiral in the floor design, visually connecting its two separate areas. As Brabo explains, "Some of these illustrative devices are literal, while others are looser and more evocative." Either way, the jurors found it made for a program that accurately and imaginatively reflects Nike's diverse product line.

1. Model for retail store and construction barricade.
2. Entry to retail store with Michael Jordan statue.
3. Men's fitness pavilion.
4. Nike Town exterior facade.
5. Construction barricade.
6. Tennis pavilion with terrazzo floor.
7. Aqua pond pavilion with changing exhibits and displays.

1.

Client: Nike, inc., Beaverton, OR
Design firm: Nike Design, Beaverton, OR
Barricade designers: Gordon Thompson, Allan Brabo (project architect); Alan Colvin (graphic designer)
Nike Town designers: Gordon Thompson (creative director); Richard Elder, Michael Mankowski, Alan Colvin, Michelle Melandri, Randy Poulson, Gena Gloar (designers); Anne Bond (archives); Rebecca Kotch (visual merchandising); Bob Lambie (copywriter)

2.

3.

4.

5.

6.

7.

Nike 'Campus'

The assignment was expansive: Nike's 74-acre, $187-million "campus,"—with eight buildings and 570,000 square feet of office space—needed a comprehensive interior and exterior program of directional and identification signage. The designers responded by first analyzing what elements might best express the company's corporate culture and its philosophy, one that stressed high design, innovation, and simplicity. Even the fact that Nike used the term "campus" instead of "headquarters" suggested to the designers a shift in attitude, from the traditional corporate environment to a setting that includes research and casual fun.

The design team determined that both strong, thrusting vertical forms, like the "swoosh" of the Nike symbol itself, and curved, perforated surfaces were clear references to architectural elements of the campus itself. "Since these also reflected design elements in the company's products, they became the foundation of our program," explain the designers. "We also felt that the layering of different materials could be used to express the character and even look of Nike shoes and clothing."

The "Stop" sign created by the designers typifies the layering of forms, images, and textures used throughout the numerous program elements. The face of the sign—a brushed stainless steel surface with laser-cut letters—is a curved form that relates to the curve of the company symbol. Behind the face is a flat, red plane in 3M reflective vinyl. Three curved, horizontal fins connect the sign to two aluminum, vertical posts. These posts, painted black, have a crisp edge that refers to similar vertical elements inside the buildings.

Nike's corporate typeface, Futura Regular condensed 78 per cent, was specified for all identification and directional signs. The palette was restricted to black, Nike red, white, and natural metal finishes, making for a crisp and contemporary look that supports the corporate image.

The all-encompassing program not only included the more obvious informational and directional signs, but extended also to fire alarm pulls, athletic event challenge ladders, recyclable waste containers, fire hydrants, and roadway crossing markers. In addition, the designers created a specialized location directory to various tributes to athletes on the campus, and a directory of contributors to the design and construction of the campus.

While the Casebook jurors could not help but be impressed by the sheer scale of the program, they questioned whether that scale was really necessary. "Isn't this a little oppressive, a little overdone?" asked Virginia Gehshan, and Jim Biber found that "There are too many ideas here that don't add up." All the same, for the program's meeting such an ambitious challenge, jurors voted in favor of its inclusion in the Casebook.

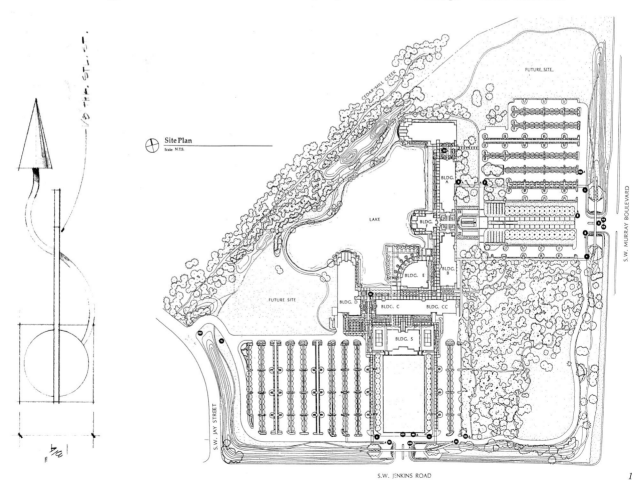

Site Plan
Scale: N.T.S.

2.

3.

4.

5.

6.

7.

1. Site plan of campus.
2. Overpass graphics.
3. Brushed stainless steel, laser-cut STOP sign.
4. Rear view of STOP sign reveals layering.
5. Roadway identification.
6. Fire lane identification.
7. Handicap access signage.

8.

9.

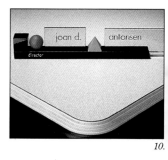

10.

Client: Nike, Inc., Beaverton, OR
Design firm: Design Partnership/
Portland, Portland, OR
Designer: Kenneth G. Ambrosini
Architect: Thompson Vaivoda &
Associates, Portland, OR
Fabricator: Vomar International, Inc.,
Sepulveda, CA

11.

12.

13.

14.

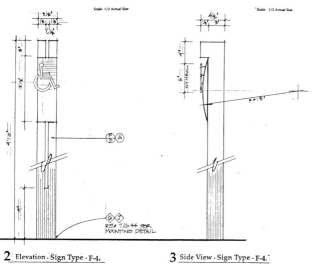

2 Elevation · Sign Type · F-4.
Scale: 3" = 1' - 0"

3 Side View · Sign Type · F-4.
Scale: 3" = 1' - 0"

15.

8. Room identification.
9. Series of signs used in day-care facility.
10. Desk signs.
11. Site plan.
12. Café entrance sign.
13. Building entrance identification.
14. Parking lot signage.
*15. Elevation and side view drawings of
sign types.*

Environmental Graphics/16

Fernbank Museum of Natural History

1. Night view of building entrance.
2. Cast concrete main identity sign.

1.

The style of this museum, completed in 1992, perpetuates the age-old tradition of museum architecture. It is a grand and monumental public space, and its signage is integrated into the architecture as a "single, seamless design statement," says Jon Roll, principal of the design firm behind the style.

The program included all identification, direction, and regulation signage; a hand map; and two interior friezes. Throughout, Roll's low-profile approach abounds: For example, there is no sign above the entry arch; Roll felt that the architecture made the

necessary, sufficient announcement in this semi-rural environment. Also, on all interior signage, a subtle palette based on the white, gray, and beige wall colors reinforces the sense of integration.

Casebook jurors found the two interior friezes especially compelling and appropriate. These were intended to evoke the 19th-century museum tradition of presenting information in such grand and decorative sequences. In the lobby, one frieze, featuring the historic (and evocative) names of some of Georgia's rivers, lakes, and other natural

2.

phenomena—Chatahoochee, Okefenofee, and Ocmulgee, for example—suggests a strong civic presence. The other, in the Natural History Hall, is a collage of plant and animal forms—cut from foamboard and lit from the rear—that is at once dramatic and restrained.

The silhouetted forms of

the flora and fauna frieze are consistent with other elements of the program, also meant to be read in profile. As Roll explains, "The building itself was designed to be read in profile." Bodoni Roman, then, was the typeface used throughout, selected for its elegance and profile legibility. Also, the flat serifs of Bodoni reflected the horizontal reveals in the walls.

PVC panels were specified throughout the program both for the friezes and sign plaques. They provided a clean edge for saw-cut letters and could be easily bent to conform to wall curvature.

3.

While the designers were satisfied with the implementation of their program, they feel that additional elements might have strengthened it further. Specifically, dinosaur topiary on the front lawn and hanging sculpture in the Great Hall and dining area were suggested—graphic devices that reflect the spirit of the museum without spelling it out literally. These were not ultimately adopted because of budget restraints and a concern that they would make the program feel "overdone." In the end, it was perhaps the right decision: This sense of elegant restraint is exactly what Casebook jurors and museum visitors remarked upon.

4.

3. Cutout foamboard frieze featuring plant and animal forms.
4. Foamboard frieze in lobby reciting regional names.

5.

6.

7.

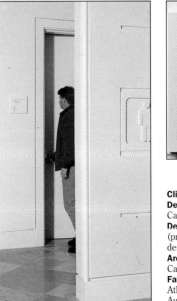

8.

Shell Exhibit
IMAX
Theatre

9.

Client: Fernbank, Inc., Atlanta, GA
Design firm: Jon Roll & Associates,
Cambridge, MA
Designers: M J Wuest, Denise Lugar
(project designers); Rafael Weil (staff
designer)
Architect: Graham Gund Architects,
Cambridge, MA
Fabricators: Designers Workshop,
Atlanta, GA; Metal Specialties, Inc.,
Austell, GA

5. Backlighting adds drama to silhouettes
of frieze.
6. Overhead screenprinted foamboard
directional sign.
7. Saw-cut letters in PVC panels of theater
sign.

8. Men's room signage.
9. Foamboard room sign with routed
reveal.

The Salad Bowl

That a fast food restaurant could take its cues from the fine arts might seem like a stretch, but the Casebook jurors agreed that it worked here. The graphics program for this New York City eatery, which opened during the blockbuster Matisse exhibition at the Museum of Modern Art, evokes all the color and exhilaration of French pottery and Matisse cut-outs. The 5000-square-foot space—long, narrow, and windowless—called out for a low-budget treatment of drywall and paint. But the imaginative result, featuring 12'-high salad bowls painted with impressionistic fruits and greenery, adds up to much more.

Fiberglas was initially specified for the bowls but was cancelled because it could not be delivered on schedule. How, then, to construct the shapes? Ultimately, they were made from a series of metal ribs to which thin strips of drywall were bolted. The curved forms were then spackled and painted with murals of cut-out shapes. The smaller one, in shades of blue, recedes slightly, suggesting a sense of false perspective, and giving the appearance of greater depth to the space. On the other hand, the larger bowl, in yellows, appears to come forward more assertively. In combination, they create a high-impact solution on a low budget.

Indeed, budget and schedule restrictions demanded that the designer, Susan Roberts, "cut to the chase." While the simplicity of the murals is engaging and appropriate, they were also designed to be painted—using Liquitex Artists' Acrylics—in less than two weeks by Roberts and only one assistant.

The program also included a 10'-square neon entrance sign animated by similar cut-out shapes. "My type books were all back in Georgia, so I used an Art Deco typeface out of a Dover type book," Roberts explains. "I selected it because it has a round 'O,' which I could replace with a head of lettuce or onion, and because of its thin stroke, which translates well into neon."

She attributes the success of the program in part to a strong working collaboration with the architect. "I incorporated my knowledge of typography, color, and visual communication skills with the architect's architectural systems, lighting, spatial and sculptural knowledge. We had known each other for 17 years and have an easygoing relationship based on humor, respect, and responsible scheduling." It is, to be sure, a sensible list of ingredients for any environmental graphics program.

Client: The Salad Bowl, New York, NY
Design firm: Susan Roberts: Art Color Design, Athens, GA
Designer: Susan Roberts (graphic designer/muralist/colorist)
Architect: Hugh Boyd/Boyd Associates, Montclair, NJ
Fabricators: Hamilton Woodworking, Blairstown NJ; Commercial Stainless, Bloomsburg, PA; The Lighting Practice/Alfred Borden IV, Philadelphia, PA; Alfred de la Houssaye (pear sculpture), New York, NY

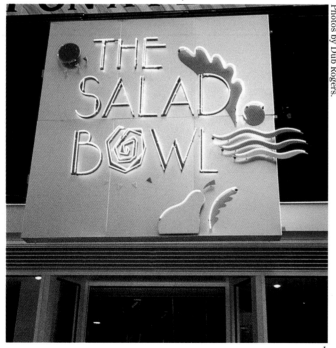

Photos by Dub Rogers.

1.

2.

1. Neon entrance sign with cutout shapes.
2. Salad bowl with mural.
3. Blue salad bowl in rear of room recedes.
4. Painted yellow salad bowl.

"My firm wasn't retained. We volunteered to join a committee," designer Hannah Alderfer of New York's HHA Design emphasizes, and her statement represents the broader commitment behind this project. Working on a low budget of $5000 over two months, the volunteer designers put together a highly visible program for the 1992 presidential campaign that addressed a broad range of women's issues, including violence against women, childcare, reproductive freedom, and the ERA.

Alderfer explains that the designers were looking for "a movable, very large format with multiple and changeable messages." Billboards and posters, then, wouldn't do it. Instead, images were computer-generated and outputted as transparencies, to end up as 8"-by-10", glass-mounted slides—47 in total, some in Spanish. These were then projected at night as 40'-by-60' images on the sides of buildings in Houston and New York. In addition, with the projector mobile-mounted, the images were shown from a truck as it toured the streets. A soundtrack of voices and music accompanied the projections, making for provocative street productions.

To keep costs down, the designers depended on found images, so picture research took the place of new photography. While this did keep expenses down, it presented its own challenges. It was difficult for the designers to find imagery that was culturally diverse yet politically relevant. Also,

persuading well-known photographers to allow their work to be used and manipulated free of charge required time and effort.

All the images were found in black-and-white; the designers brought color to the program by both coloring the photographs and using color type. (The only color not used was red, because of its poor projection quality.) Some designs were rendered on the computer, while others were designed "from scratch."

The designers also wrote the slogans—rendered in over 30 typefaces, mostly sans-serif for better readability when projected. "We wanted diversity instead of unity," explain the designers.

The purpose of the program was not simply to generate awareness of women's issues, but to encourage women to speak out themselves in an exercise of empowerment. Specifically, this meant inviting women to get up in front of an open microphone after the slide presentations. Many of these women had never spoken publicly before, but told poignant and compelling stories about the inequities facing them in daily life.

The Casebook jurors commended the program for delivering its own strong message in an efficient way, and agreed that the scale suited its political statement. The program conveyed all the strength of a project that came from the heart, proving that innovation need not carry a large price tag. "This is just beautifully done," summed up one juror.

1.

2.

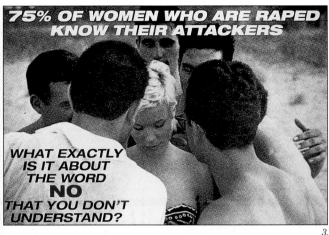

75% OF WOMEN WHO ARE RAPED KNOW THEIR ATTACKERS

WHAT EXACTLY IS IT ABOUT THE WORD NO THAT YOU DON'T UNDERSTAND?

3.

Photo courtesy of The Bettmann Archive

LESS THAN 10% OF ALL SEXUAL HARASSMENT VICTIMS EVER COME FORWARD

NO WONDER

4.

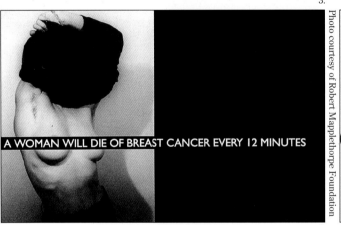

Photo courtesy of Robert Mapplethorpe Foundation

A WOMAN WILL DIE OF BREAST CANCER EVERY 12 MINUTES

5.

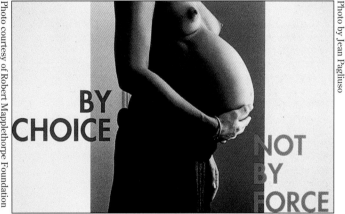

Photo by Jean Pagliuso

BY CHOICE NOT BY FORCE

6.

AS A CHILD I KNEW I WAS A LESBIAN

I DIDN'T KNOW I'D BE HATED FOR IT AS AN ADULT

7.

$33.7 Million on Weapons every hour

$2.9 Million on Education every hour

NATIONAL SECURITY?

8.

1. Street production at night.
2. Pro-choice image and audience.
3–8. Diverse political and social messages of program.

Client: Women's Action Coalition
Design firm: The Houston Visual Committee, Houston, TX
Designers: Hannah Alderfer, New York, NY; Marybeth Nelson, New York, NY
Projectionist: Robert Collier/ Technique Mirage, Atlanta, GA

Begun in the late '60s, Cincinnati's Skywalk System, now connecting some 15 city blocks, is one of the country's oldest overhead walkway networks. While that may be to its credit, its outdated and incomplete signage system was not. How, then, to redesign and retrofit the existing signage?

As the designers explain, "Our goal in redesigning the system was to provide orientation for tourists, shoppers, and citizens as to what the system is, the businesses located on it, and the relationship of the system to downtown Cincinnati. At the same time, we wanted to establish a sense of place and to communicate the city's character and history."

To do all this, the designers first invented a new logo to identify the Skywalk path and entrances throughout the system. Deciding that the tight letter-spacing of the original Helvetica typeface compromised legibility, they replaced it with Univers 67. The partial outline of a cloud and a series of dots, meant to represent the walkway, were added, yielding a 3-D effect and enhancing identity. "The touch of cloud is nice," commented Casebook juror Jon Roll. "It works."

The designers then overhauled the entire signage system. Dividing the city into five districts, they identified each on maps and directional signs with photographs and pictograms—picked up from graphics developed for the city's Bicentennial celebration—of the districts' major landmarks. Two-sided street-level markers orient users to their present location, indicate the nearest Skywalk entrance, and, along with the landmark illustration, convey historical information about the city. On the Skywalk level, there are four kinds of markers: two-sided freestanding, four-sided freestanding, five-panel wall-mounted, and three-panel wall-mounted. These are directional, guiding users through the system.

The designers specified Skywalk Match Blue as the background color for all markers because it represents the sky and provides a strong contrast to the urban streetscape. A darker blue, PMS 5405, was used on all overhead signage and as a secondary color for markers.

Typography, now updated to Univers 57 and 67, was PMS white.

While the new signage system meets the broader needs of contemporary users, it is, in fact, not altogether new. Mindful of both economy and environmental concerns, the designers recycled the original '70s signage system by removing the aluminum panels from their steel frames, sandblasting them, spraying them with automotive paint, and then re-silkscreening them. It was an approach that represented the spirit of the entire program, which combined an appreciation for the existing signage with the recognition that a more contemporary urban landscape needed to be accommodated.

1.

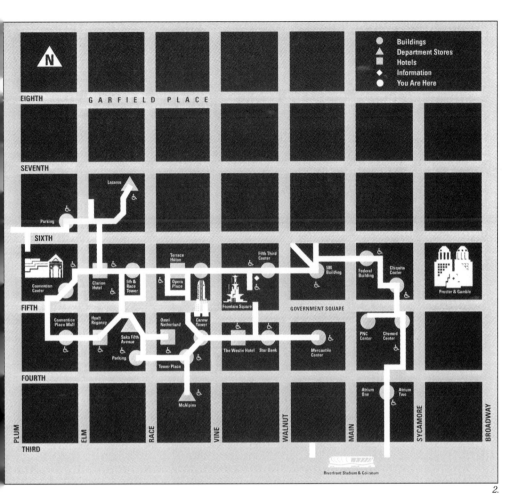

2.

Buildings
Department Stores
Hotels
Information
You Are Here

EIGHTH GARFIELD PLACE
SEVENTH
SIXTH
FIFTH
FOURTH
THIRD

PLUM ELM RACE VINE WALNUT MAIN SYCAMORE BROADWAY

Lazarus
Parking
Convention Center
Clarion Hotel
5th & Race Tower
Opera Place
Terrace Hilton
Fifth Third Center
580 Building
Federal Building
Chiquita Center
Procter & Gamble
Hyatt Regency
Convention Place Mall
Omni Netherland
Carew Tower
Fountain Square
GOVERNMENT SQUARE
PNC Center
Chemed Center
Saks Fifth Avenue
Parking
Tower Place
The Westin Hotel
Star Bank
Mercantile Center
Atrium One
Atrium Two
McAlpins
Riverfront Stadium & Coliseum

1. New logo—with cloud outline and walkway below.
2. Map of Skywalk system.
3. Original 1977 Skywalk signage.
4. 1984 Skywalk design.
5. Current Skywalk design.

3.

4.

5.

Vine Street   Skywalk   Fountain Square ↑

6.

6. Skywalk strip sign, plate-mounted.
7. Skywalk strip signs.
8, 9. Two-sided street-level markers with architectural images.
10. Four-sided Skywalk level marker.

Convention Center ↑

7.

Client: City of Cincinnati
Design firm: Graphic Design Section, Office of Architecture, City of Cincinnati, OH
Designers: Marcia McGinnis Shortt (design director); Ric Snodgrass, Laura Martin, Laura Curran, Lucy Frueh (design and production); Edwin Frey (designer); Dutro Blocksom (photographer for markers)
Architects: Robert H. Richardson, Denise Rohrer
Fabricators: Geograph Industries, Cincinnati, OH

8.   9.   10.

Loeb Supermarkets

In supermarkets, packaging design and the grocery displays themselves often compete with store graphics, which—as a result—can appear confusing and beside the point. Casebook jurors found the signage system for Loeb's Inc., a supermarket chain in Canada, to be exactly the opposite, a more calculated program that was at once informative and enlivening.

The design objectives were to create the atmosphere of an outdoor market, with its fresh foods and spontaneity, and to differentiate the various departments. To meet both ends, the designers specified the construction of canvas awnings, supported by steel or aluminum armature, throughout the store. Though actually permanent, these sculptural awnings in various shapes and sizes convey the lively and impromptu environment of a street market, while identifying the different food departments in a highly visible manner. That they are modular components also made them easy to specify for new stores and to retrofit for existing ones.

The system was altered in one department, Ready Loeb, which sells the store's own brand of prepared foods. Here, oversize photographs, along with the occasional cartoon character, depict people of all ages enjoying the department's various selections. These photos further emphasize the overall lively atmosphere.

The designers also used color to differentiate various departments: green (Pantone 362C) signage, for example, in the produce department; red (200C) in Ready Loeb; and orange (165C) in baked goods. Throughout most of the store, Univers 75 and Fenice typefaces were selected for their readability and overall consistency with the design criteria; these, the designers say, included "brightness, efficiency, freshness, distinctiveness and a contemporary quality." In the Ready Loeb area, a diversity of type contributes to the street market feeling. The jurors concluded that the program did, indeed, bring such a feeling to life.

1. Entrance and exterior signage at night.

1.

2.

3.

4.

5.

6.

2–4. *Series of canvas awnings.*
5. *Overhead panels.*
6. *Photographic mural.*
7. *Displays for baked goods.*
8. *Check-out lanes.*

7.

8.

Client: LOEB, Inc., Gloucester, Ontario, Canada
Design firm: Lippincott & Margulies, Inc., New York, NY
Designers: Raymond Poelvoorde (creative director); Joan Ellison (environmental designer); Connie Birdsall (graphic designer); Wayne Van Verspoor (designer)
Architect: Berns Farrow Architects, Inc., Ottawa, Ontario, Canada
Fabricators: Screen Print Industries, Inc., Brantford, Ontario, Canada
Lighting consultant: Sara Schrager, Ridgefield, CT
Ready-wall Photography: Kenneth Willardt, New York, NY
Photographer: Andre Beneteau/Acme Photographic, Toronto, Ontario, Canada

Anyone who has ever had a rough morning knows that coffee can be a divine gift; such was the utterly credible premise of the graphics program for a small diner in Manhattan. Witness the memorable logo, in which a steaming cup of coffee has been accessorized—indeed, elevated—by a halo. The designers explain that "Our clients stressed they didn't want to make the diner retro or trendy; they just wanted to reveal the beauty of the simple, honest food they offer at a fair price."

Both the interior of the 3000-square-foot diner and its graphics set out to establish exactly that beauty of the ordinary. A series of 12 slightly different clocks, staples of old-time diners, hangs over the counter. Naugahyde upholstery was specified for stools and banquettes, and three types of linoleum cover the floors and tabletops. A preliminary plan to continue this use of "tacky" surface materials, including fake brick, marble, and knotty-pine veneers on square columns interspersed through the space, was abandoned because of the cost.

Architect James Biber succinctly sums up the credo for the program: "Everything's average; nothing matches." But while the design celebrates the ordinary, it is obviously not at the expense of the occasional Big Idea, as the connection between coffee and spirituality attests. In another instance, four framed photostats—of a salt shaker, a matchbook, a teabag, and a wire whisk—hang in the dining room, where they are intended to evoke the four primal elements—earth, fire, water, and wind.

The power of design often comes from how deeply it taps into universal assumptions. Surely the saintly coffee cup logo—repeated on menus, announcements, signage, stationery, matchbooks, and even a baseball cap—does just that. Casebook jurors and users of the diner agree that while they have all suspected the presence of a halo, only rarely has it been sighted with such certainty, grace, and good will.

1.

2.

3.

4.

5.

6.

7.

1. Clashing colors of Naugahyde stools.
2. "Coffee as saint" logo.
3. Exterior signage.
4. Entrance awning with logo.
5. Promotional matchbooks.
6. Logo on baseball cap.
7. Bannister reiterates diner name.

8.

9.

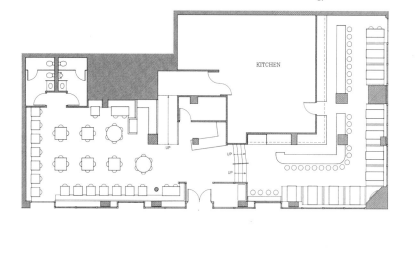

KITCHEN

42ND STREET

UP

UP
UP

ELEVENTH AVENUE

10.

8. *Archetypal diner objects as art.*
9. *Framed photostats of primal elements reinterpreted.*
10. *Diner floorplan.*

Client: Gotham Equities, New York, New York
Design firm: Pentagram Design, New York, NY
Designers: Michael Bierut; Lisa Cerveney (assistant graphic designer)
Architects: James Biber; Michael Zweck-Bronner (assistant architect), New York, NY
Illustrator: Woody Pirtle

Jefferson High School Commemorative Installation

Designer B.J. Krivanek conceived of this installation during an early planning visit to Jefferson High School in South Central Los Angeles. "After seeing some students led out of the principal's office in handcuffs, I met with him to discuss the project. At a school in what is perhaps this country's most embattled inner city, the installation was designed to honor the achievements of Jefferson's most prominent graduates. More to the point, however, was its powerful message to current students—that they, too, could become achievers.

Located in the lobby outside the school auditorium, which is the most community-oriented space on the campus, the exhibit displays photographs of distinguished graduates such as Dexter Gordon, Alvin Ailey, and Nobel laureate Ralph Bunche. Rather than simply glorifying these role models and thereby possibly distancing them from

students viewing their photographs, the exhibit has assembled the group in a more egalitarian, human way. Interspersed among the 15 photographs are mirrors, so that students can envision themselves as members of this all-star lineup. Jurors found the simple sense of humanity here compelling, and considered this image continuum an example of how a simple, straightforward design solution can communicate a resonant message.

The exhibit was designed to complement the streamlined Moderne style of the campus, built in the mid-'30s. Aluminum, a material that evokes the Futurism of that decade, was specified for structural forms. The photographs themselves are protected by thick sheets of acrylic. Neon lighting—a wash of green on the wall behind the aluminum structure and pale orange

1.

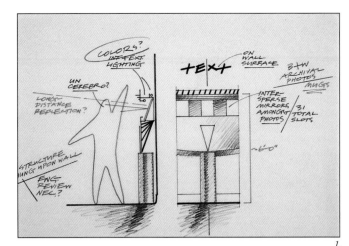

Photo by Jesse Milden

2.

1. Preliminary installation sketch.
2. Exterior of "Moderne" style campus.
3. Early fabrication drawing.

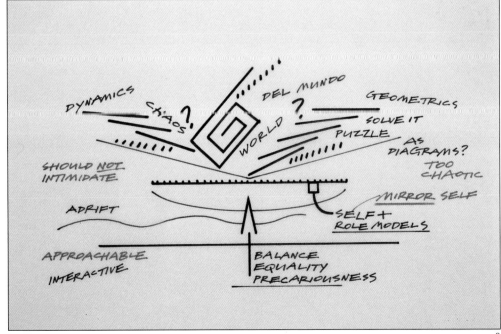

3.

illuminating the photos within—was also selected as a period reference. Inscriptions, precison-cut from brushed aluminum, are predominantly in Futura. Says Krivanek, "I chose to design an installation generated from both the historical presence of the building and the collective memory of the community, and to restore a sense of dignity and purpose to this embattled educational environment."

Krivanek worked on a limited budget, indeed largely on a pro bono basis. Of the total $15,000 allocated for the program, only 10 per cent went toward design services. "As there was no funding for design development," the designer explains, "many decisions were based on gut-level feelings." If restoring a sense of dignity is integral to any inner city design program, this installation succeeds. It respects the existing architecture and confers dignity on past graduates. Most notably, however, is that the project communicates the potent message that this dignity can be shared by the new generation of students.

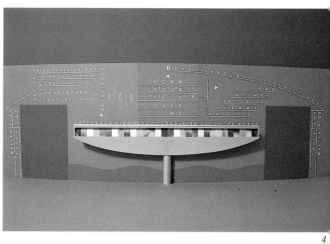

4

Client: Jefferson High School of the Los Angeles Unified School District, Lo Angeles, CA
Design firm: BJ Krivanek Art+Design, Los Angeles, CA
Designers: B.J. Krivanek (principal/design director); David Rieger (studio assistant)
Photographers: Edmund Barr, Jesse Milden
Fabricator: AHR Ampersand, Glendale, CA
Neon illumination: Neonics, Marina Del Rey, CA

FULL•ELEVATION

Scale: 3/8″ = 1′ - 0″

DREAM•LEARN•ORIENT•
DECIDE•CONS—DER•TURNING•PO—INTES•
DESTINATION•
•CROSSROADS•
•JUNCTURE•CHOOS

MAZE•ENTER

YOU

B R E A K • T H R O U G H • T O • Y O U R • F U T U R E •

FORM
LIYBOEURRTY
CASLELLIFNG
OVER
TIME

ESTEEM
TRIUMPH
PROGRESS
DREAMS
ABILITY

MASTER•PLAN EDUCATION

EDUCATION MASTER•PLAN

•JEFFERSON•HIGH•SCHOOL•GRADUATES•OUT•IN•THE•WORLD•

ABCDEFGHIJ
KLMNOPQR
STUVWXYZ

ABCDEFGHIJ
KLMNOPQR
STUVWXYZ

A▶
B   B

5.

BJ•KRIVANEK
ART&DESIGN

COMMEMORATIVE•ART
AND•INSCRIPTION•INSTALLATION

Jefferson High School • Auditorium • Los Angeles, California

Copyright 1989 • BJ Krivanek • All Rights Reserved

6.

7.

4. *Installation model.*
5. *Elevation drawing of installation.*
6. *Completed installation.*
7. *Viewer of—and participant in—installation.*

Design in any medium is often a matter of beginning with something usual—an image, a material, a process—and doing something unusual with it. Such was the case with the donor-recognition system at the Art Center College of Design in Pasadena, California. Designer Dennis Scott Juett explains the approach: "Because the pencil represents the fundamental tool used by every student at Art Center, it was chosen as the central image for the program."

While an appropriate icon for an art school, the pencil is also an image that lends itself to a signage program that is continually changing. Because donor gifts are totaled cumulatively, repeat donors are constantly moving to higher gift categories. Each "pencil," then, contains an interchangeable, colored cap and matching colored lead—gold, silver, bronze, red, violet, blue, green, or yellow—that signifies the donor's giving level and can be changed without replacing the entire unit. Aside from its inventive use of the pencil image, the program was cited by Casebook jurors for being easily and inexpensively updated and expanded.

The body for each pencil unit is milled out of hexagonal aluminum and anodized black. The tapered end is then remilled to remove the anodizing, leaving a shiny taper. At that point, the donor's name is etched into the black anodized surface.

Four metal cases, each containing five vertical display units, were installed in the wall itself. The display units are outfitted with internal lighting and evenly-spaced stand-offs to hold the pencils.

The program also included an accessory to be given to each donor: a duplicate of each pencil, presented in a custom wood box. Like the pencils on the wall, these can be upgraded by different colored end caps and lead as the donor's cumulative gift advances to higher levels.

Just as unusual as the program was the process behind it. The donor wall was, in fact, designed by Juett, while he was still an Art Center student, for a course in graphic design. After evaluating the pencil concept, school administrators asked him to further refine the

1

2.

design and develop a budget. He did so, and just days before his graduation, the president and trustees of the college approved both. Managing all aspects of fabrication, assembly, and installation, Juett completed the project in nine months after graduation, in time for a benefactors' dinner celebrating the successful completion of a $25-million fund-raising campaign. Soon afterward, he became a partner in his father's design firm.

Client: Art Center College of Design, Pasadena, CA
Design firm: Dennis S. Juett & Associates, Inc., Pasadena, CA
Designer: Dennis Scott Juett
Fabricators: Sign Pac (display cases), Costa Mesa, CA; Sign Designers (pencil end caps), San Gabriel, CA; Decorative Glass Processes (sandblasting), Monrovia, CA; Dimension Seal Products (O-rings), Los Angeles, CA; Gene's Gun Drilling (pencil manufacturer), Los Angeles, CA; Kandle King (wax leads), Pomdale, CA

1. Display cases built into donor wall.
2. Pencil, gift box, and pedestal donor gift package.
3. Donor recognition signage and display unit.
4. Vertical display units with color-coded pencils.

3.

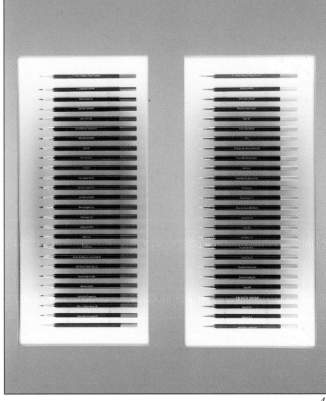

4.

1.

2.

1. Exterior view of campus and
Administration Building.
2. Stone-carver working on marble
entrance gateway.
3. One-point perspective of campus
looking south.
4. Administration Building lobby.
5. Lecture hall.
6. Medical Education Center commons.

The beauty of this program was that it tended not to be noticed. People just used it, assuming it had always been there, which was exactly how designer Jon Roll wanted it. The traditional stone carving he selected appears as if it is part of the original 1906 architecture, rather than a contemporary addition. Indeed, respect for historic precedent governed the program throughout.

While the intent, according to Roll, was to orient and inform students and visitors, it was "above all to enrich the academic environment of a prestigious institution," Boston's Harvard Medical School. The graphics program included exterior signage, entry portals, building and room identification, directories and directional signing, and donor recognition for the diverse components of the 90-year-old campus, which includes the classic marble buildings of the quad, the new Genetics Research Building, the AIDS Research Center, and the student-residence facility.

Roll specified traditional stone carving, wood carving, metal casting, and other crafts he felt would be consistent with the rigorous academic spirit of the campus. Entrance portals, then, were hand-chiselled,

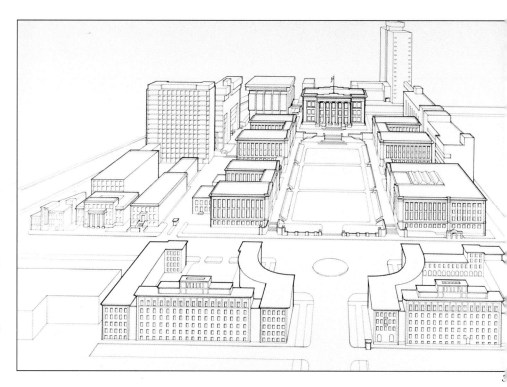

4.

5.

suggesting both permanence and tradition. The Greek cross motif used by Shepley, Rutan, and Coolidge in the original campus architecture was sandblasted on interior doors. Elsewhere, the medical school seal was cast or etched in bronze or handcarved on oak medallions. Garamond was the typeface used throughout the program, selected for its elegant and handsome letterforms. All the craft mediums suggest that, rather than being components of a new, uniform system, the graphics evolved throughout the history of the campus— making for an effect that Roll calls "graphic memory." That the program often goes unnoticed suggests that Roll has been successful.

Beyond the challenges that come with craft disciplines, which demand a high level of expertise, there was the issue of addressing the individual program of each building while maintaining a sense of graphic continuity. Roll points out that this was accomplished by tight control over uniform typography, use of the medical school shield, and the centered format, while materials and fabrication processes were allowed to evolve individually with each building.

To Roll, the most satisfying aspect of the assignment was gaining an understanding of the superb craftsmanship that went into the original buildings—and then designing a graphics program that could resonate with the character and workmanship of that earlier time.

6.

7.

8.

16.

9.

10.

11.

12.

13.

14.

15.

Client: Harvard Medical School, Boston, MA
Design firm: Jon Roll & Associates, Cambridge, MA
Designers: Jon Roll, Sharon Stafford
Architect: Ellenzweig Associates, Cambridge, MA
Fabricators: Frankie Bunyard (carved graphics), Boston, MA; APCO Graphics, Atlanta, GA; Design Communications, Boston, MA

7. Entrance portal, Vanderbuilt Hall.
8. Close-up of shield for lecture hall.
9. Room identification sign.
10. Level identification sign.
11. Library identification sign.
12. Room identification sign.
13. Donor recognition plaque.
14. Signage for student room.
15. Library identification silkscreened on glass with sandblasted Greek cross pattern on reverse side.
16. Entrance to Quad and Medical Education Center.

The Gas Company

Photo by Annette Del Zoppo Photography

As is often the case with environmental graphics, this program began with building identification and quickly broadened to encompass vehicle graphics, signage for regional facilities, uniforms, and print materials. Not that this was surprising considering the client: The Southern California Gas Company is the largest public gas utility in the U.S., with some 30,000 employees and 96 branch facilities.

The corporate graphics program was initiated with the completion of the company's 54-story headquarters in downtown Los Angeles. Along with building signage and identification, it included a logotype, symbol, and a color and typographic system. The designers first updated the client's logo and symbol, a blue flame intended to represent clean-burning fuel. They also suggested a name change to "The Gas Company," nomenclature conveying a friendlier and more accessible presence.

Designers at Sussman/ Prejza rejected the corporate convention of spelling out the company name at the top of the building as an outdated and unnecessary intrusion on the urban landscape. Instead, they looked to the pedestrian level, where they placed perhaps the most inventive component in the program: the 3-D, abstract flame sconces around the building's exterior. These sconces of color-washed aluminum, along with aluminum sculptural flame chandeliers, installed in the building's two entry lobbies, are a more subtle and tasteful expression of corporate identity. Both sconces and chandeliers went through numerous preliminary mock-ups. As the designers explain, "We did a number of these, testing color, paint, and reflective surfaces before finding the shape that reflected the light the way we wanted."

Signage in the building is consistent with the crisp and somewhat abstract imagery of the sconces. For the aluminum sign panels throughout, the designers specified a palette of silver (aluminum, stainless steel, or paint), black, white, and blue. Silver was reserved as a background color, and blue was used either for background or, consistent with the company's traditional use of the color, for details in the flame. All typography— Steel Futura that the designers found representative of both the building's character and the company's corporate image— was rendered in black-and-white.

1. Exterior with sign and sconces.
2. Flame sconces on building exterior.

Photo by Annette Del Zoppo Photography

Photo by Annette Del Zoppo Photography

3.

Photo by Nick Merrick/Hedrich Blessing

THE GAS COMPANY TOWER

EXIT   ENTER

4.

FLOOR **L**

EMERGENCY
Exit Plan

Photo by Sara Kaplivsky

5.

6.

3. Interior chandelier.
4. Parking garage signs.
5. Interior emergency exit sign.
6. Close-up view of sconce.
7. Single flame chandelier in lobby.
8. Vehicle graphics.
9. Interior tenant sign.
10. Stationery graphics.

Client: The Gas Company, Los Angeles, CA
Design firm: Sussman/Prejza & Co., Inc, Culver City, CA
Designers: Deborah Sussman (principal-in-charge); Scott Cuyler (associate-in-charge)
Architect: Skidmore, Owings & Merrill, Los Angeles, CA

Photo by Annette Del Zoppo Photography

Photo by Nick Merrick/Hedrich Blessing

7.

8.

Photo by Sara Kapilivsky

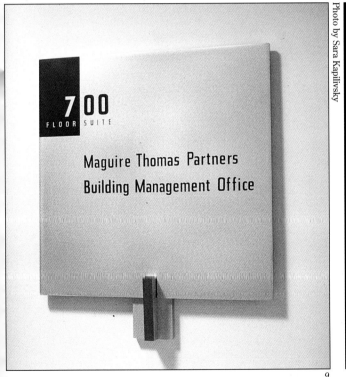

700
FLOOR SUITE

Maguire Thomas Partners
Building Management Office

Photo by Nick Merrick/Hedrich Blessing

9.

10.

Rather than focusing on exotic specimens of water life, the new Tennessee Aquarium investigates the ecosystems of the Tennessee Valley, a three-state region defined by the circuitous Tennessee River. If the river is the story line, as the designers suggest, then the characters are the fish and their habitats. The designers approached the diverse subject matter with a graphics program that has its own diversity of images and mediums.

The identity symbol for the aquarium, then, has a stylized image of the river running through it—its path expressed by a broad white line, with thinner lines suggesting tributaries. Outlines depict a variety of aquatic and bird life, all in fluid forms consistent with the river image. the overall circular shape of the symbol suggests the totality of an entire self-supporting ecosystem. Consistent with the overall program, the fluid Garamond Italic typeface was specified.

The program also included typographic murals based on the names and characteristics of the species found in the rivers and lakes of the valley. Developed on a Macintosh program, typefaces were distorted to evoke distinctive features of the various species, making for a display that is at once informational and humorous.

A similar spirit is found in the lobby of the aquarium's theater. Here, large-scale, vinyl, die-cut shapes, in a simple bright green color, were applied to the wall, making an informative and engaging display of various Tennessee leaf types. Around the aquarium's entry lobby winds a ribbon frieze citing the evocative names of Tennessee towns; below are photo murals of the state's lush landscape. These murals are mounted on triangulated panels such that visitors see one when passing from left to right, and the other when passing in the opposite direction.

The most expressive display, however, is found in a dramatic fiber-optic ceiling sculpture, suspended over the aquarium's central 128'-long,

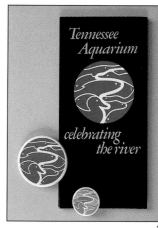

1.

2.

3.

4.

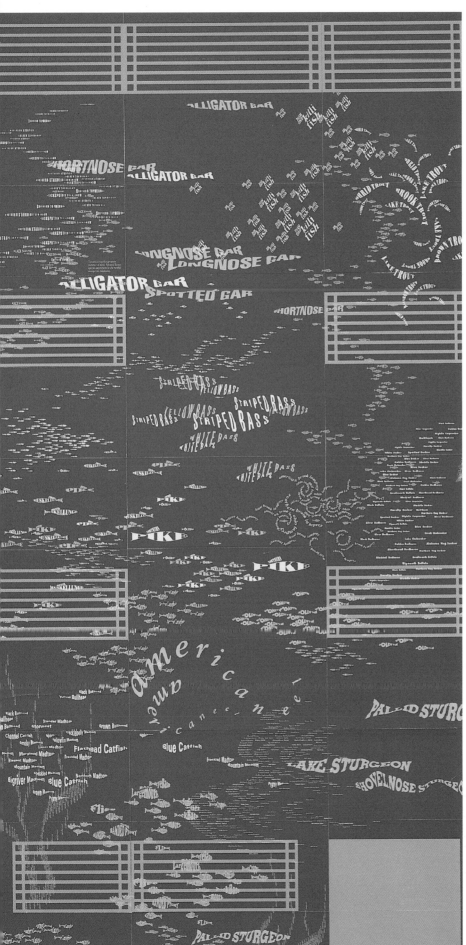

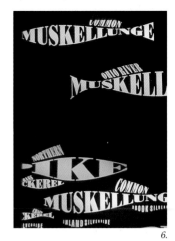

6.

1. *Exterior view of aquarium.*
2. *Interior exhibit signage.*
3. *Logo drawing.*
4. *Aquarium logo.*
5. *Typographic mural.*
6. *Detail of typographic mural.*

5.

24'-wide "canyon." This space, defined by walls of internally illuminated fish tanks, houses ramps and viewing platforms. The sculpture animates the ceiling with a continuum of light—actually a series of ¼" fiber-optic cables stretching the full length of the space. Sixteen illuminators, concealed along the ends of the space, light the total of 13,000 feet of cable.

The sculpture's constantly undulating patterns of light and color evoke the continuum of a river, this one overhead—exactly where it should be to reinforce the underwater exhibits. The Casebook jurors agreed that it was this river of light that transformed the program from a lively and educational display series to a more memorable and visceral experience.

7

8.

9

7. Theatre lobby with leaf cutouts.
8, 9. Entry lobby with ribbon frieze.
10. Fiber-optic ceiling sculpture.
11. Assortment of wave patterns.
12. Drawings for fiber-optic display.

Client: Tennessee Aquarium, Chattanooga, TN
Design firm: Chermayeff & Geismar, Inc., New York, NY
Designers: Tom Geismar, Ivan Chermayeff, Keith Helmetag, Cathy Schaefer
Architect: Cambridge Seven Associates, Cambridge, MA
Fabricators: Cummings Sign Co., Nashville, TN (major sign); Maltbie Associates, Mt. Laurel, NJ (wall graphics); Art & Technology, Inc., Burbank, CA (ceiling light sculpture)

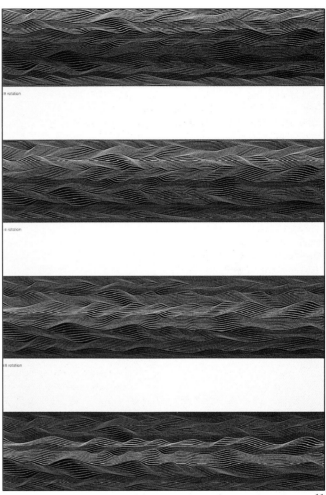

10.   11.

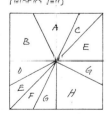
WHEEL FOR GROUP 1
(FIBERS 1-9)

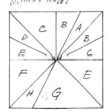
WHEEL FOR GROUP 2
(FIBERS 10-18)

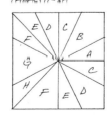
WHEEL FOR GROUP 3
(FIBERS 19-27)

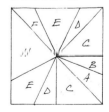
WHEEL FOR GROUP 4
(FIBERS 28-36)

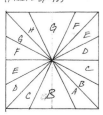
WHEEL FOR GROUP 5
(FIBERS 37-45)

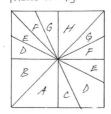
WHEEL FOR GROUP 6
(FIBERS 46-54)

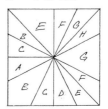
WHEEL FOR GROUP 7
(FIBERS 55-63)

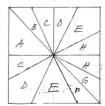
WHEEL FOR GROUP 8
(FIBERS 64-72)

12.

*WHEELS ROTATE ONCE EVERY 15 SECONDS & ARE SYNCHRONIZED.

Seven Hills Park

The Casebook jurors were engaged by the whimsical iconography of the program for Seven Hills Park, a half-acre park in the city of Somerville, Massachusetts. In a prominent location with a subway entrance at one end, the underutilized site needed an identity program. The design objective, the designers explain, was "to create a public historical park, a stimulating, kinetic, educational space that would enliven and create a landmark for the city." Jurors agreed that the chosen imagery—including an old nunnery, a stone fortress, an eccentric weathervane, and a clock tower—did exactly that.

To meet their objective, the designers created seven sculptures, ranging in height from 30' to 50', which refer to the history and development of Somerville, built on seven hills. "We wanted to embrace the city and its people," they explain. Thus, each sculpture represents one of the hills, and together they engage the entire community. While these sculptures are making historical references, they also work as vibrant and very contemporary urban markers.

After exploring the city's history to determine the appropriate imagery, the designers developed an extensive series of scale drawings, sight-line studies, full-size color comps of all typographic information, and finally, half- and full-size mock-ups of each sculpture, conveying how it would appear once installed. The biggest problem came after this process, when they were called upon repeatedly to re-evaluate the placement of the sculptures. "When digging began, we ran into all sorts of surprises that had not been documented in any city plans. So, then we'd go back to the drawing board, lay out the sculpture again, go back to the site, stake it out, and the process would start all over again," the designers explain.

Because each sculpture weighed between 1000 pounds and two tons, the designers worked closely with an engineer to determine the layout and support structure. To accommodate the sculptures, brick bases with steel supports were embedded into underground concrete bases. A granite cap—with the hill's name carved into it—was installed on top of the base, from which four steel columns emerge. The columns in turn support a square, aluminum cap, which hides a spinning mechanism. Finally, the sculpture, carved from high-density foam, spins above the columns. The typeface used is Matrix, chosen for its legibility.

The budget precluded postdesign studies to evaluate the program. Its designers, however, report that both their client and users of the park have supplied them with ample verbal praise—to which the Casebook jurors have added their own kudos.

1.

2.

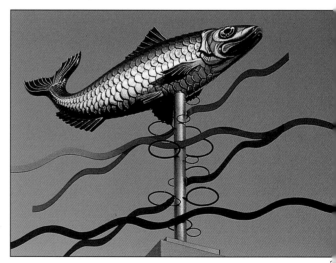

3.

1–3. Details of sculptures.
4. View of park with sculptures.

5.

Client: City of Somerville, MA
Design firm: Clifford Selbert Design, Cambridge, MA
Designers: Clifford Selbert, Ruth Loetterle, Robin Perkins
Consulting engineers: Joan Rumbaugh Engineering, Cambridge, MA; R.P. Manzilli & Co., Newton, MA
Fabricators: Amidon & Co., Sandwich, MA; Cornelius Architectural Products, Pittsburgh, PA
Contractor: Paolini Corp., Newton, MA

6.

5, 6. Details of sculptures.

Toronto's SkyDome

Opened to the public in June 1989, Toronto's SkyDome is the world's first solid-structure, retractable-roof stadium. Both its roof and flexible seating enable it to accommodate football games, concerts, and political conventions in any season, with equal ease. The objectives for its environmental graphics program included development of a comprehensive signage system to direct some 50,000 people through the circular building; a visual identity based on a "sky" theme; guidelines for future strategies; and additional projects, such as souvenir kiosks, automated banking facilities, and banners.

While the designers satisfied these objectives, they may have been most insightful in identifying and minimizing the traditional problems of stadium environments—not least of all the concrete landscape and garish advertising. The graphics program confronted both of these, incorporating them into an approach that set out to integrate art, architecture, and advertising.

"Various visual and verbal interpretations of the sky were appropriate design directions, given the retractable roof and desired identity theme," they explain. Clouds, stars, the sun and the moon, rendered in a full spectrum of colors, provide the imagery.

All interior signage consists of modular, lightweight, perforated aluminum screen panels above a neon strip. While concealing the HVAC and electrical infrastructure, these screens aid in wayfinding and incorporate a back-lit billboard advertising system. A series of banners promotes the sense of celebration, bringing visual relief from the concrete landscape.

Because the program was backed by an inadequate budget, the designers' solution was actually conceived as a revenue generator as well: The program's advertising billboards ultimately paid for the signage. As they point out, "This not only solved the budget issue, but resulted in a less cluttered, highly integrated, and thematically unified approach to stadium signage." The Casebook panel agreed.

1.

1. SkyDome Stadium exterior with CN Tower in background.
2. Flags and banners above one of the entrances.

2.

3. Interior restroom signage.
4. Interior directional sign.
5. Close-up of a sky element graphic.
6. Directional sign band runs along entire interior while overhead screens display graphics of sky elements specific to sections of stadium.
7. Manual for graphic application control.
8. Directional sign band and cloud graphics.

3.   4.   5.

Client: Stadium Corporation of
Ontario, Toronto, Ontario, Canada
Design firms: Gottschalk+Ash
International, Toronto, Ontario; Keith
Muller and Associates, Toronto,
Ontario
Designers: *Gottschalk+Ash:* Stuart Ash
(partner and senior designer); Peter
Adam, Brenda Tong, Robert Jensen,
Diane Castellan, Katlin Kovats
(designers); *Keith Muller:* Keith
Muller (partner); Randy Johnson,
Larry Burak, David Tonizzo, Joanne
Crone, Robert Ketchen (designers)

7.

8.

"Finally, some humor," sighed one Casebook juror in relief. Indeed, the jurors all agreed that this program was unusually humorous for a shareholders' meeting, and they appreciated its attempt to stretch the context of these ordinarily staid events.

The atmosphere of the annual meeting, which attracts some 7000 attendees, is, according to the designers, a cross between a political convention and a corporate pep rally. The objectives of the graphics program, then, were to convey energy and enthusiasm and create a group "event," while directing large numbers of people through a confusing space. "Think Team," an approach reflecting the question-and-answer format of the company's annual report became the theme for the event.

To communicate the message of teamwork, the designers used blow-ups of vintage black-and-white photographs (with halftone dot patterns that created their own lively graphics) of various "teams" from fields such as music, sports, and science. From the mouths of these team players came incongruous, unexpected, and humorous bubble messages having to do with the company's corporate statement. One doesn't expect water-ballet dancers to be discussing corporate strategy.

The typefaces selected for the bubble messages were Trixie and Bell Gothic, the former specified because it had been used in the company's annual report. "We wanted an immediate playful look," the designers explain. The red, black, and white

1

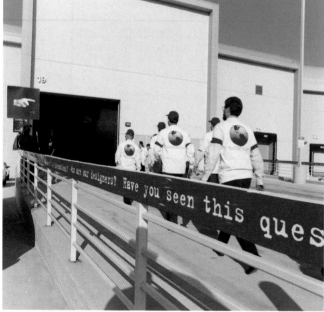

2.

3

color palette, while the unofficial corporate colors, also conveyed a sense of drama and excitement.

The oversize photographs were complemented with a series of red plastic ribbons. While these were imprinted with their own series of provocative questions, they also served as a trafficking device. As environmental elements, the ribbons were consistent with the sometimes provocative architecture of the new convention hall, designed by architect Peter Eisenman, in which the meeting was held.

The ribbons comprised one of those small design elements that far surpassed the expectations of the designers. "We knew the ribbon would be a flexible element," the designers recall, "but the dynamics between the ribbon and the environment still managed to surprise us. For instance, unbeknown to us, a large globe sculpture in the public space intruded on our environment. One swooping gesture with the ribbon around its equator immediately incorporated the globe into our event."

The opinions of the panel of jurors was slightly mixed; Jon Roll, for example, questioned whether the program wasn't visually a bit amateurish. In the end, however, it was exactly this unexpected simplicity and humor in a business environment that won the program a place in the Casebook.

4.

5.

6.

1. Red ribbon as accent to exterior architecture.
2. Red ribbon used to support traffic flow.
3. Blow-up photograph of team players.
4. Bubble messages installed in conference hall.
5, 6. Team players issuing advice in circulation areas.

Client: The Limited, Inc., Columbus, OH
Design firm: Frankfurt Balkind Partners, New York, NY
Designers: Laurel Shoemaker, Robert Wong; Sarah Oman (project director); Robin Giles (project coordinator); Tina Moskin (production manager); Kent Hunter (creative director)
Architect: Peter Eisenman, New York, NY
Consulting organizations: Joyce Barnes Wolff/Mills Janes Productions, Hilliard, OH; Ric Wanetik and Associates, Columbus, OH

7.

8.

9.

7. Globe sculpture tied with red ribbon.
8. Restroom signage.
9. Vintage photograph in circulation area.

Oriole Park at Camden Yards

In an age of electronic scoreboards and contemporary crowd-control needs, it's no small feat to bring a sense of nostalgia to the design of a ball park, but that was the goal established by the designers of Oriole Park at Camden Yards, home of the Baltimore Orioles. Designer David Ashton explains that their mission was to develop an environmental graphics program that would be "in keeping with baseball as the great American sport." And the Casebook jurors agreed that this had been accomplished. "The graphics support the ball park," one observed. Added another, "This is not sterile."

The scale of the program ranged from a small promotional brochure to a six-story scoreboard. Other components included advertising panels, main and perimeter entry signage, stadium and team logos, banners, and ushers' uniforms.

The designers launched their ten-month schedule for the program by immersing

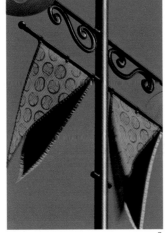

1. View of main scoreboard.
2, 3. Colorful exterior banners.
4. Oriole weathervane.

5.

themselves in the ball team's historical documents—old uniform catalogs, biographies of players, a history of the team, and books on older, cherished baseball stadiums such as Brooklyn's Ebbets Field. Working with these, the designers initiated an identity program that evokes the sentimental history of baseball. Old-fashioned typefaces were custom-designed, and a traditional color palette of green, red, black, orange, white, and blue was adopted. Oriole weathervanes and a clock are further accents that bring a sense of history with them. All of these, however, are loose translations of historical design elements and motifs, a suggestive amalgamation rather than precise reproductions.

While the jurors agreed that baseball tradition was clearly evoked here, they questioned whether it was, in fact, too nostalgic. "Why can't we invent something a little more contemporary?" asked Jim Biber. On the other hand, is there any way to do ball park graphics without being nostalgic? That quibble aside, the jurors agreed that for all the old-fashioned sentiment, there is an equal amount of energy and exuberance appropriate for a more modern-day program.

6.

7.

8.

9.

10.

11.

12.

13.

5. Oriole weathervanes and clock.
6. Main entry signage.
7. Usher's uniform.
8. Directional sign.
9. Medallion sign installed on preview center for All-star week.
10. Pavement inset.
11. Perimeter signage.
12. Advertising panel.
13. Hall-of-Fame sculpture.

Clients: Baltimore Orioles, Baltimore, MD; Maryland Stadium Authority, Baltimore, MD
Design firm: David Ashton and Co. Ltd., Baltimore, MD
Designers: David Ashton, Garv Cieradkowski, Jessica Koman
Architect: Helmuth, Obata & Kassabaum, Kansas City, MO
Fabricators: Triangle Sign, Baltimore, MD; Tom Moore, Glen Rock, PA
Consulting engineer: Tigue Lighting, Philadelphia, PA

Disney's East Coast Corporate Headquarters

1.

Disney's East Coast corporate headquarters occupies 401,000 square feet on four floors and contains some powerful visual themes—namely, the world's largest sundial and, of course, the world's most famous mouse, Mickey. The building had been designed by Arata Isozaki, whose work is marked by symbolism. Isozaki felt strongly that the theme for the office complex have to do with the passage of time. So, aside from Mickey Mouse, the central focus of the headquarters is an immense cone at the core of the building—actually a sundial. Isozaki relied upon a complete interior and exterior signage program to clarify his message.

None of this threw the design team. As member Tracy Turner explains, "Isozaki's incredible architecture was full of color, shape, pattern, and scale. In order to work with the architecture, capture the spirit of Disney, and have a clear and legible sign program, we decided to keep all the signage black-and-white, using a circle, or Mickey 'ear,' as the predominant and consistent design element." The circle is also in synch with the abstract forms used by Isozaki in the building complex, including the sundial and circular drive.

The circle format proved to be flexible enough for the comprehensive program, which included major and minor building identification, entrances, directory pylons, lobby directories, and department and room identification. Exterior directional signs, for example, were 26" aluminum disks, painted black with vivid triangles of color indicating direction; interior directional signs were the same size with cutouts. The typeface throughout is Optima Bold and Roman, specified because it is consistent with the classic plan of Isozaki's building and the signage done for the overall site and roadways by Sussman-Prejza.

The designers also incorporated various quotes about time—such as Einstein's observation that "Time is what a clock measures"—into the program. These are etched into black granite and set into white marble blocks at eight different points along the complex's circular walkway.

In the end, though, it was probably Mickey's ears that did it. "I just like the ears best of all," sighed Casebook juror Ken Carbone. For all of their stark and elegant geometry, they are, after all, just mouse ears, which makes for an engaging incongruity.

2.

3.

4.

5.

1. Mouse ears at main entrance.
2. Circular stop sign—soon to be octagonal.
3. Two black circles used for primary identification.
4. Circular metal cutout directional sign.
5. Traffic directional sign.

Client: Disney Development Company Orlando, FL
Design firm: Tracy Turner Design, Inc., New York, NY
Designers: Tracy Turner (principal); Graham Uden (senior designer)
Architect: Arata Isozaki & Associates, Tokyo, Japan
Fabricators: McCurdy Shea Architectural Fabricators, Tampa, FL

7.

8.

6. Pylon identifying sundial.
7. Building directory with acrylic disk.
8. Sundial Court informational sign.
9. Courtyard sign.
10. Room identification sign.
11. Paver in courtyard with sandblasted quotation.

9.

10.

11.

"This may be the best thing I've seen," Casebook juror Jim Biber remarked. "It's gorgeous," added juror Virginia Gehshan. The object of their enthusiasm was a permanent exhibition animating and altogether transforming the narrow hallway entrance to the Corning Corporation's international headquarters in New York City. Such a long, narrow corridor might have been perceived as a negative element, but instead it became the stage for a vibrant light show that demonstrates both the company's pioneering work in fiber optics and its more poetic applications.

Glass and light were both the subject and media here. In approaching the materials, the designers were thinking in terms of a metaphorical expression. "We approach problems metaphysically as well as environmentally," they explain. And applying such thinking to the Corning assignment allowed them to be particularly inventive. The transmission of light is a major component of the company's past and present business. The designers' wall of light was intended to express both Corning's past innovations in light transmission and the spirit of future developments.

The exhibition was an active combination of computer-controlled point-source light, dichroic filters, prisms, and mirrors—the light patterns of each focused along the 50' wall. Different dichroic filters separate light into its various colors along the visible spectrum; by carefully selecting the filters and aiming them through mirrors and prisms, a varying array of patterns was created. Their ultimate effect is to paint and repaint the hallway with an ever-changing light show. Color patterns and hues, at once dramatic and subtle, are continually altered at a slow but perceptible rate controlled by computer.

Clearly, in this interior landscape up-to-the-minute light science has become an expressive symbol, which, of course, was the intent of both client and designer. Simultaneously poetic and precise, the wall, as metaphor for the company, was so appreciated by the client that Corning ultimately asked the designers to add a brief text caption, so their creation would be shared more fully with visitors. The designers describe the work as an "artful, engaging presentation that communicated the essential aspects of Corning's corporate values wrapped in a memorable, visual experience," and the Casebook jurors agreed unanimously that the program is totally appropriate on all levels.

1. Corridor entrance with light show.

Photos by Wolfgang Hoyt

CORNING
Corning Incorporated
Steuben Offices

2. Detail of wall of light.
3. Patterns created by light transmissions.

Photo by Wolfgang Hoyt

Client: Corning Corporation, Corning , NY
Design firm: Donovan and Green, New York, NY
Designers: Michael Donovan, Allen Wilpon, Susan Berman
Architect: Kevin Roche/John Dinkeloo & Associates, Hamden, CT
Fabricators: Maltbie Associates, Mt. Carmel, NJ

Ristorante Ecco

Each year's Casebook offers up a sentimental favorite—usually a small project that nevertheless manages to captivate the jurors. This year, the $1200 graphics program, completed in two months, for San Francisco's Ristorante Ecco may be that project. In particular, jurors found the informal sensibility of the program's hand-lettered logotype quite appropriate to the rustic ambience of this restaurant

The logo and identity program included site banners, business cards, menus, matchboxes, and entry and wayfinding signage. The logotype, therefore, had to be adaptable to different materials and scales: a 6' Corten steel entry sign with laser-cut lettering; stitched nylon banners outside the restaurant; a main doorway of sandblasted glass; and 2" matchboxes. The designers explain, "The materials were chosen as a related family of rich surfaces for various applications of the logo," and the jurors pointed out that the interplay of these surface textures further contributes to the restaurant's rustic atmosphere.

The jurors also noted the banners outside the restaurant. Because the main entrance is on the side, rather than front, of the building, the designers considered various options for directional graphics. Awnings were considered but rejected in favor of the dynamic, vertical presence the banners create. Perpendicular to the basically horizontal building, they have high visibility and successfully direct customers to the entrance on a small side street. And, the earthtones of their taupe and black palette is consistent with the feel of the overall program.

1. *Exterior nylon banners.*
2. *Steel entry sign.*
3. *Sandblasted glass doorway.*

2.

3.

Client: Ristorante Ecco,
San Francisco, CA
Design firm: Morla Design, San
Francisco, CA
Designers: Jennifer Morla, Scott
Drummond, Craig Bailey
Fabricators: South Park Fabricators,
San Francisco, CA; Mobius, Eugene,
OR; Martinelli Environmental
Graphics, San Francisco, CA; Doublet,
San Francisco, CA

Indianapolis Museum of Art

The good news was that when the Indianapolis Museum of Art built a new addition, it more than doubled its exhibition space. The bad news was that, as is often the case in expansion programs, the new building made glaringly apparent the need for a cohesive signage program throughout the complex—a 152-acre urban site with a botanical garden, four art pavilions, lecture hall, theater, concert terraces, restaurants, and shops.

Says designer Richard Poulin, "This was the rare opportunity not only to develop a new graphic identity, but to establish graphic standards for the entire complex." Previously, there was no consistent identity in directional or informational graphics, and publications were designed on an ad hoc basis. What was needed was a cohesive identity. It was that simple, and quite extensive. The museum was looking for a comprehensive design program, covering all architectural graphics and sign elements, exterior banners and site signs, stationery, brochures, a monthly magazine, all promotional print materials, shopping bags, and interpretive graphics for the museum's major collections.

After three months of extensive research, the designers developed a sign schedule with a complete listing of all sign types, and their locations, quantities, and proposed wording. From this, they produced a group of sample signs, in the process selecting typography, sizes, color, and materials. The final

Indianapolis Museum of Art

3.

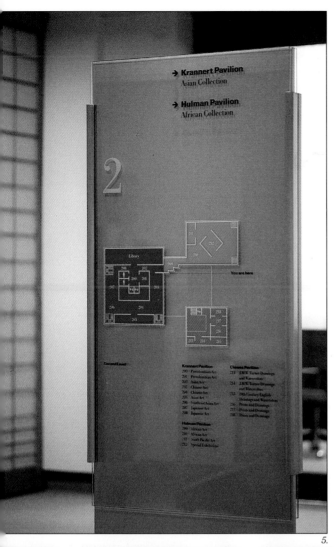

1. Logotype/symbol.
2. Exterior main identification sign.
3. Site banners.
4. Exterior aluminum kiosk.
5. Satin-finish aluminum informational kiosk.
6. Promotional material.
7. Exterior aluminum kiosks.
8. Promotional materials.

5.

6.

7.

8.

9.

10.

11.

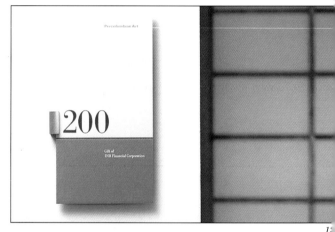

12.

13.

14.

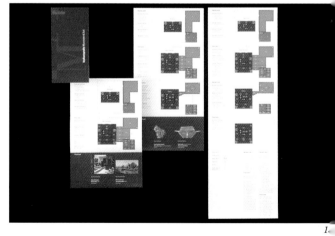

1.

9. Pavilion identification sign.
10. Dimensional wood letters used for gallery identification.
11. Promotional shopping bags.
12. Gallery/donor identification sign.
13. Conference room sign.
14. Room identification sign.
15, 16. Promotional print materials.
17. Interior information kiosk.
18. Art caption.

product was marked by great variety—dimensional stainless steel letters; etched, gold-leaf, tempered glass panels; sub-surface silk-screened Plexiglas panels; baked aluminum panels with reflective Scotchlite vinyl die-cut letters; silk-screened, brushed aluminum panels; and gold leaf on glass.

The Casebook jurors were especially appreciative of the program's well-integrated typography. The designers had specified two typefaces as an organizational device: Sans-Serif Univers was used for all non–fine art information, such as directional signage, and Bodoni Antiqua was used for all information regarding artworks, such as caption labels and gallery identification.

The palette—burgundy, turquoise, and ocher—was developed to convey information as well, with each color symbolizing one of the three pavilions. Krannert, housing American art, is represented by Burgundy; Hulman, with Oceanic art, by turquoise; and Clowes, with Renaissance art, by ocher. This palette was used for directional signage throughout the complex. The jurors agreed that such applications of color and typography made for a beautifully executed program.

Client: Indianapolis Museum of Art, Indianapolis, IN
Design firm: Richard Poulin Design Group Inc., New York, NY
Designers: Richard Poulin (project director/designer); Kirsten Steinorth, Debra Drodville (project designers)
Architect: Edward Larrabee Barnes/ John M. Y. Lee & Associates, New York, NY
Fabricators: Cornelius Architectural Products, Pittsburgh, PA

16.

17.

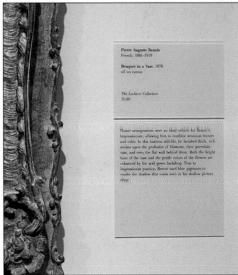

18.

Occupying a 70-acre parcel of land along the Santa Ana Freeway, Tustin Market Place is made up of a number of retail stores surrounding a "village center" of specialty shops, movie theaters, and restaurants. "The complex," the designers explain, "was to be such an oversized project that the architect said people should be 8' tall and drive huge trucks to shop here." The design goal, then, was a signage and identity program, including entry monuments, project colors, and tenant signing, that would convey the full scale of the center.

With 1700 feet of freeway footage, it was clear from the start that the program would be oriented toward the freeway, making sightlines, scale, and sequencing of the utmost importance. The first part of the program, then, addressed the signage to be viewed from the freeway, including exposure for ten major tenants. Along with this, the program included signs that would be viewed both from the public streets inside and on the visitors' eye level.

While the designers recognized the significance of the nearby freeway, they also acknowledged the powerful architectural statement—unusual for a retail center—made by the complex's sequence of buildings, designed by Ricardo Legoretta. Their solution, therefore, was to integrate the signage into the architecture with a system of aluminum panels that not only created a strong profile when viewed from the freeway, but also played off the massiveness of

the buildings. The panels themselves have been covered in a surface texture resembling stucco.

The designers also created a unique halo of white neon light over the complex, with colorful neon accents where major tenants had their "towers"; this halo illuminates and identifies the complex at night. The logotype is an altered Futura extra-bold with somewhat squared, blocklike letters that are consistent with the squared forms of the architecture.

Originally, the designers had considered a brighter palette more consistent with the strong colors used in the architecture. The city, however, found the strong colors overbearing and asked the architects to revise the scheme. A more somber palette resulted all-around, with purple, black, and white used throughout the design program. The designers themselves still question whether the original colors would have made the program more whimsical and festive, further animating the complex. They explain that "A successful retail project generally needs some sort of visual activity besides its architecture." Ultimately, though, the design team was satisfied, as were the Casebook jurors, who valued the unusual degree of integration between architecture and signage.

1

1. Main vertical entry sign.
2. Long shot of project.
3. Pylons at night.
4. Main horizontal sign.

2.

3.

4.

5.

7.

6.

Client: Donahue Schriber Developers, Newport Beach, CA
Design firm: Sussman/Prejza & Co., Inc., Culver City, CA
Designers: Deborah Sussman, Scott Cuyler, Holly Hampton, Corky Retson
Architect: Ricardo Legoretta, Mexico City, Mexico
Fabricator: Coast Sign Display, Inc., Anaheim, CA

5. Retail pylons.
6, 7. Directional signs.

Hotel Hankyu International

Graphic designers often complain about identity programs being given all the attention of an afterthought. Not so here. What distinguished this identity program for a flagship luxury hotel in Osaka, Japan, was that it was commissioned before other parts of the design; graphic elements were actually intended to guide the development of the hotel's interior design and architecture. Beyond that, the client merely directed, in a briefing before design began, that the program develop "a distinctive emblem that would communicate quality, internationalism—read 'not japanese'—and the universal appeal of flowers," says art director Michael Gericke.

The program was to include signage, room folders, stationery, packaging, menus, and other guest amenities. Because the project was so inclusive and would influence the subsequent interior design, the designers first constructed a prototype hotel suite. Throughout the year-and-a-half timetable, they continually "checked into" this sample suite to review interior colors, finishes, furniture, signage, and all the print graphics that were to be used in the hotel rooms.

Working this way, the designers proceeded to develop a system of six stylized flower symbols—one for each floor—and a custom alphabet to be used with them. The flowers themselves have been rendered in a faintly Art Deco style, by now surely its own international language. These symbols can be used in a variety of ways, making for a

1.

2.

1. Series of six flower logos.
2. Room identification panels.

program both unusual and flexible. The color palette used throughout the program was white, purple, gold, and a metallic green, all specified because the designers found these both elegant and easy to reproduce on a wide variety of materials, including paper, stone, metals, and leather.

For signage, the designers developed custom English and Japanese typefaces, specifying Garamond No. 3 for all English text. As the designers did not read or speak Japanese, working with Japanese typography posed problems. These were solved by retaining the services of a consultant design firm in Osaka that could handle the implementation and mechanical artwork for all pieces with Japanese text. Such a spirit of exchange was essential to the success of the program, and it was what the designers most valued in the end. Indeed, they recall that the cross-cultural exchange and experience designing for a different cultural environment were the most satisfying aspects of this project.

3.

4.

5.

6.

7.

8.

9.

10.

Client: Hankyu Hotels Corporation
Design firm: Pentagram Design, New York, NY
Designers: Colin Forbes, Michael Gericke (art directors), Donna Ching (designer)
Consultant design firm: OUN Design Corporation and Dentsu, Inc., Tokyo, Japan
Interior designers: IntraDesign, Los Angeles, CA
Illustrator: McRay Magleby, Provo, UT

3. Brass newspaper holder with doorbell and message light.
4. Primary entrance signage.
5. Directional signs.
6. Luggage tag.
7. Restaurant and cocktail lounge accessories.
8. Bathroom amenities.
9. Graphics on linens and towels.
10. Gift packaging for room amenities.

Mickey's Toontown

While most signage programs aim to deliver information, those coming from the studios of Walt Disney Imagineering are more concerned with delivering punch lines. That was certainly the case with the 400 or so items of signage created for Mickey's Toontown. This new Magic Kingdom suburb, the hometown of Mickey and his animated colleagues, isn't simply a set, according to Dave Burkhart of Walt Disney Imagineering, but a living, breathing, three-dimensional cartoon environment. "Everything is exaggerated to convey the cartoonish elements," says Burkhart. "For example, there are no straight lines or conventional architecture here."

The signage program—ranging in scale from pieces only 2″ long to those 10′ high and 30′ wide—is consistent with the eccentricities of this animated landscape. All its elements, including major and secondary marquees, directional and informational signs, menus, show support such as labels and logos, and vehicles, share the soft edges, simple shapes, and inflated quality of the town's cartoon geography.

The team of 12 graphic designers worked closely with the project architect in order to follow the style of the town, which had been designed to suggest the colorfully painted backgrounds of classic Disney cartoons. The graphic elements reflected this painted look, conforming to the Toontown palette of 26 principal colors. All visible surfaces were designed as

1. Populated streets of Toontown.
2. Mickey's Toontown main marquee.
3. "Toon Hole" cover.
4. City Hall marquee.
5. Power house facade.

4.

5.

obvious simulations of the real thing; woods, metals, and stonework, for example, were sculpted and painted to conform to an overall consistent texture. Typography varied, though OPTI Pueblo was used repeatedly for its easy readability and visual consistency with the cartoon format.

"Unlike typical cities," explains one of its designers, "Mickey's Toontown encourages its visitors to touch, pinch, tickle, jump on, and otherwise interact with its overstuffed, animated buildings and wacky cartoon characters." That being the case, materials and construction methods needed to withstand constant assault. Most signs were constructed of fiberglass-reinforced plastic, which was cast or framed over sculpted, high-density sign foam and attached to a heavyweight stainless steel armature. Very accessible signs were often one-piece aluminum castings. And wherever possible, individual signs were backed up with hidden safety cables and secondary support structures.

The designers describe their overall theme as "whimsical, cartooney, and child-oriented." That they achieved their objective was made clear in comments made by Casebook jurors such as Jim Biber, who said simply, "Exactly appropriate, such enjoyment."

6.

7.

8.

9.

10.

11.

12.

13.

14.

15.

16.

17.

18.

6. Cartoon-style street signs.
7. Traffic sign.
8. Go-Coaster marquee.
9. Gym marquee.
10. Clock repair sign.
11. Chip & Dale mailbox.

12. Traffic sign.
13. Donald Duck mailbox.
14. Go-Coaster ride marquee.
15. Trash can decal.
16. Official Toontown seal.
17. School marquee.
18. Telephone sign.

19.

20.

21.

22.

23.

Client: The Walt Disney Company/
Disneyland, Burbank, CA
Design firm: Walt Disney
Imagineering, Glendale, CA
Designers: Mickey's Toontown team,
Graphic Design Department, Walt
Disney Imagineering, Glendale, CA
Architect: Mickey's Toontown team,
Architecture Department, Walt Disney
Imagineering, Glendale, CA

19. Dog Pound facade.
20. Fireworks Factory facade.
21. Restaurant marquee.
22. Courthouse sign.
23. Bank marquee.

When KQED Inc., a public radio and television company, consolidated its studio and administrative facilities, it moved into a three-story, low-rise warehouse with an assertive, Modernist style. During the building's renovation and redesign, the architects remained true to this vernacular. Their strongest statement was an exterior architectural fin—the extension of a bold, ocher-colored, sloping wall that pierces a third-floor atrium. A reference to historic theater marquees, this exterior fin displays stainless steel letters identifying the studio.

The mandate for the signage program was clearly one of drama and elegance, but also one of low cost. Because KQED is a nonprofit organization, it was imperative that the design acknowledge budget restrictions and avoid even the appearance of extravagance. All the same, because the building itself was the result of a major capital campaign, recognition of donors was also part of the design mandate. The donor recognition components were, in fact, "the most visible and important programmatic graphic elements."

The Casebook jurors did find the "donor recognition floor" particularly inventive and compelling. The tile floor of the reception area (originally specified as terrazzo, but changed to linoleum tile to adhere to the budget) was embedded with a grid of stainless steel donor name rings, each 6" in diameter. As the designers explain, "This became an architectural statement celebrating the individuals and groups that contributed to a special building-construction fund." In addition, a donor-recognition wall in the third-floor, central public space was studded with 8" white glass disks, screen-printed with still other names. The jurors found both solutions elegant, efficient, and inexpensive.

Graphics were treated elsewhere as a logical extension of the architecture. The circular motif of the donor rings was continued in department and room identification signs. All such wall signs were simple, painted-acrylic shapes with silk-screened graphics, which required neither complex nor expensive fabrication. Ocher, yellow, dark eggplant, off-white, and gray, along with the natural appearances of the dominant stainless steel and glass, made for a distinctive color palette.

Futura typefaces, consistent with the Modernist style of the architecture, were used throughout. Snell Roundhand Script was specified as well on selected signage; the designers felt that its soft, curvilinear detail was a subtle reference to the dramatically angled and bowing atrium wall. This thoughtful approach to the type characterized the entire program: throughout, graphic elements were logical, appropriate to the architecture, and—at the same time—capable of making their own strong design statement.

1.

2.

1. Exterior architectural "fin" signage.
2. Acrylic wall disk.

3.

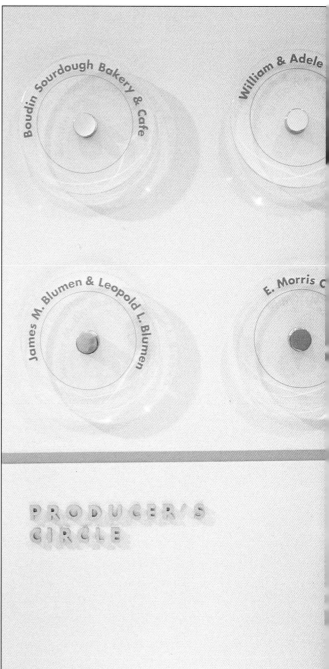

4.

5.

6.

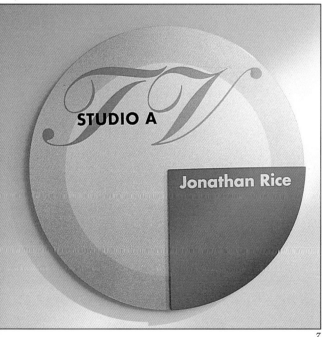

7.

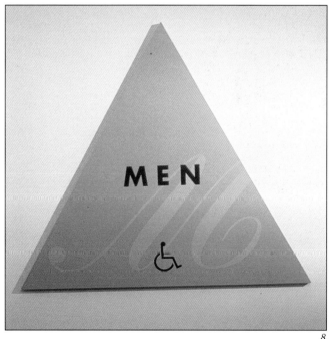

8.

3. Donor recognition floor with name rings.
4. Detail of donor recognition wall with glass disks.
5–7. Variations on silkscreened acrylic wall disks.
8. Men's room signage.

Client: KQED Inc., San Francisco, CA
Design firm: Gensler and Associates/ Graphics, San Francisco, CA
Designers: John Bricker (design director); Tom Horton (senior designer); Julie Vogel (designer)
Architect: Gensler and Associates/ Architects, San Francisco, CA
Fabricators: Thomas Swan Sign Company, San Francisco, CA
Lighting consultant: Horton Lees Lighting Design, San Francisco, CA

When it was completed in 1991, the renovation of the Pierpont Morgan Library received critical acclaim for its sensitive re-evaluation and integration of disparate components, including its Renaissance revival building designed by McKim, Mead and White, a neoclassical annex, a 19th-century brownstone, and more contemporary garden court. Affirming this sense of synthesis was a new graphics program—signage to direct visitors through the museum, informational signs about specific exhibits, and donor-recognition signs.

Considering the diversity of the architectural program, the designers felt the graphics should be at once traditional and contemporary. A solution of simple, flat signage in bronze or acrylic was considered but ultimately discarded because it lacked the desired grace. After conducting visitor circulation studies, the designers decided that relatively few signs were really necessary; in light of that, they explain, "We decided that a more sophisticated—and expensive—solution, using custom bronze work, would be both feasible as well as most architecturally compatible."

The program, then, specified handcrafted signs for all public spaces and galleries. In the profile of a gentle arc, the signs are made of brass with three custom-finished bronze patinas, applied by hand on a unique textured background. All signs are either free-standing or pin-mounted to walls. The type—in widely spaced Bembo caps to maximize legibility for the great number of senior citizens who frequent the collection—is etched and paint-filled. To reduce costs, painted acrylic panels with subsurface, silk-screened type were used for signage in nonpublic areas.

For the benefactors' list in the contemporary Garden Court, names were carved in a limestone wall and in-filled with gold leaf. Because the final list of benefactors was not determined until late in construction, coordinating the stone carving was slightly problematic.

It was the designers' objective to invent a program that would be consistent "with the elegant and contemporary architectural renovation." The Casebook jurors classified the result as "subtle," "elegant," and "appropriate," all suggesting that the designers were successful.

1.

Client: Pierpont Morgan Library, New York, NY
Design firm: Carbone Smolan Associates, New York, NY
Designers: Kenneth Carbone, Beth Bangor, John Nishimoto
Architect: Voorsanger and Associates, New York, NY
Fabricators: Metalforms, New York, NY; Sam Shefts, Bronx, NY; Signs and Decals, Brooklyn, NY

2.

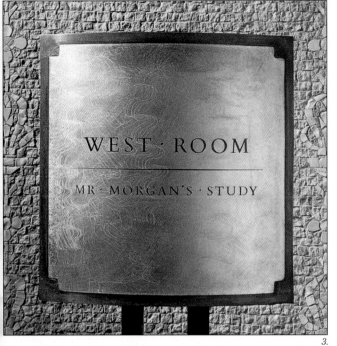

3.

4.

5.

6.

1. *Entrance signage.*
2. *Custom carved glass transom in Garden Court.*
3. *Free-standing gallery sign.*
4. *Painted acrylic wall panel.*
5. *Library floor plan.*
6. *Free-standing desk sign.*

Times Square Visitor Information Booths

A symbol of leisurely and luxurious travel, steamer trunks evoke a bygone era of elegance. The use of such an image in New York City's Times Square—with its own brand of street life, adult theaters, and crime—was unexpected to be sure. Not surprisingly, the image raised questions from the Casebook jurors, one of whom asked, "Does it work here?" Yet, as incongruous as a steamer trunk seems in this particular environment, it is just as welcome. The jurors agreed that it did, in fact, work and was a small, but lively, part in a much larger urban rehabilitation program.

The steamer trunks are actually mobile visitor information booths. Intended to be eye-catching, both their size and busy graphics render them recognizable at a distance to tourists of different nationalities. Once set up, each one—approximately 8' tall, 4 1/2' wide, and 3 1/2' deep—can accommodate two people. A second, smaller trunk, stacked on top of the larger one, gives the entire unit height and announces its presence. Constructed of plywood with formica surfacing inside and out, the trunks have anodized luminum extrusions, locks, and latches. They are outfitted inside with fans to combat summer heat and track lighting for evening operation.

The steamer trunks convey fictional histories through their surface design, based on old travel stickers. Silk-screened in a variety of bright colors and applied to the cream-colored booths, these "stickers" contribute to a program that is at once nostalgic, ironic, and even brazen. It would certainly have to be brazen to get noticed in this part of town.

1.

Client: Times Square Business Improvement District, New York, NY
Design firm: The Pushpin Group, Inc., New York, NY
Designers: Roxanne Slimack (designer); Seymour Chwast (art director)
Fabricator: Calzone Case Company, Bridgeport, CT

3.

1. *Exterior of mobile steamer trunk.*
2. *Mobile steamer trunk, closed.*
3. *Interior of steamer trunk with staff.*

Getting kids into a bookstore can be tough—especially when the bookstore is in the mall, where it has to vie for their attention with video outlets, software marts, and the alluring food court. Rising to the challenge is the graphics program for a children's bookstore at the famed Mall of America in Bloomington, Minnesota. The program is both whimsical and sophisticated, bringing the store alive with characters.

Two things were obvious from the start. First, the babies of baby boomers are a quickly-growing segment of the book market. And second, as members of this electronic age, these youngsters are more visually sophisticated than previous generations. The designers, then, devised a system of "landmarks" to lure the kids into the store and hold their attention once there. When you enter the store, you know they have every kid's book imaginable.

Constructed from maple, stained in a palette of orange, yellow, purple, green, and white, the oversize landmarks have a warm, natural feel. One, a tower, displays books and provides seating, while another, a truck, exhibits new releases. Various volumes, accompanied by story characters, fly overhead—a metaphor for how books can come alive. "Book characters are very appealing," explain the designers. "They are like old friends." The Casebook jurors especially appreciated the flying books as whimsical images and an appropriate metaphor.

But once you've gotten the kids into the store, how do you get them to go all the way to the back? One way, the designers realized, was to construct a "grove" of "book trees" in the rear of the store, which became a quieter area attractive to older kids who want to stop, browse, and read. "This market was unexpected, a bonus," the designers recall about the older kids. The jurors agreed that in this period of increasing illiteracy, bookstores designed to encourage browsing as well as buying are to be commended.

1.

2.

1. Display table near entrance.
2. Entrance.
3. Entry and window displays.

3.

4.

5.

6.

7.

4. View of flying volumes.
5. Grove of book trees in rear of store for browsing.
6. Book tower display.
7. Truck display for new releases.

Client: B. Dalton, New York, NY
Design firm: Kiku Obata & Company, St. Louis, MO
Designers: Kiku Obata (creative director); Idie McGinty, Tim McGinty (project designers); Theresa Henrekin (designer), Jane McNeely, Pam Bliss (graphic designers); Ed Mantels-Seeker (logotype designer)
Architect: James Keane, St. Paul, MN
Fabricator: Design Fabricators Inc., Boulder, CO
Consulting engineers: Nelson Rudie (structural engineer), Minneapolis, MN; Lighting Management, Inc., New City, NY

Bay Area Discovery Museum

National security is rarely a factor in museum signage, but it did figure into this program. This children's museum in the Marin highlands of northern California is located on East Fort Baker, a military installation that, though inactive, issued its own set of unusual site constraints. All ground-level signage, for example, needed to adhere to strict military codes. Also, in a national crisis, much of the museum would need to be removed from the premises quickly—so all its signage must be dismantled easily. Bay area weather imposed further design restrictions; considerations of coastline fog and wind eliminated a preliminary plan relying on solar electricity.

The museum is a hands-on, interactive learning center that attracts visitors of all ages and ethnic backgrounds. Both its permanent and changing exhibitions focus on three primary areas: the San Francisco Bay area, architecture and design, and the performing arts. Aside from observing military restrictions, the question was therefore how to develop signage for a diverse museum program that would speak to a diverse audience. As the designers explain, "The signage objective was for visitors to begin the 'discovery' experience before even entering the building, and to allow those who both do and do not read English the pleasure of discovering what environment they are about to enter."

With all this in mind, the designers specified a bright

1.

1. Whimsical museum entrance signage.
2–4. Signage mobiles used for exhibits.

2.

3.

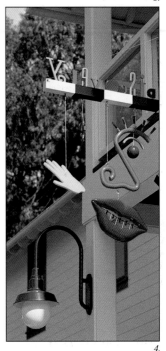

4.

system of mobiles for all skyline signage; their view was that these animated overhead sculptures could be informational while transcending barriers of language and literacy. "Mobiles are, by nature, interactive," they explain, "challenging the viewer and leading to a discovery in and of itself." Working within an eight-week schedule, the designers constructed full-scale color renderings of the eccentric and colorful assembly of objects and type forms; these were then juxtaposed next to the various buildings to determine their final sizing and placement.

Ground-level signage was animated, as well, by the use of different type styles and colored backgrounds. Military code demanded that all ground-level signage consist of conventional wooden structures currently used on military installations. The designers could, however, specify a replacement for the military brown; they chose a brighter palette, enhanced by a black-and-white checkered frieze bordering the inside top of each sign. The austere military typeface was also replaced with the warmer and more appealing Palatino.

While the Casebook jurors questioned whether the scale of the program was suited to the overall site, it was a minor quibble. In the end, they found the imagery appealing, appropriate, and indeed admirable for meeting such a unique set of site constraints.

5

5. Mobile with view of bridge.

Client: The Bay Area Discovery Museum, Sausalito, CA
Design firm: Landor Associates, San Francisco, CA
Designers: Margaret Youngblood, Rachel O'Dowd
Fabricators: Holsonback/Reification, San Francisco, CA

CALIFORNIA COLLEGE OF ARTS AND CRAFTS
ARCHITECTURE
WITHDRAWN
COLLECTION
MEYER LIBRARY